A BEGINNER'S GUIDE TO GIRL POWER!

Wannabe a

SPICE girl?

Mark Leigh
and Mike Lepine

HarperCollinsPublishers

HarperCollins*Publishers*
77-85 Fulham Palace Road,
Hammersmith, London W6 8JB

A Paperback Original 1997
1 3 5 7 9 8 6 4 2

Copyright © Illiterati International Ltd. 1997

A catalogue record for this book is
available from the British Library

ISBN 0 00 653028 1

Designed by Design/Section
Printed and bound in Great Britain by Scotprint Ltd, Musselburgh

Original photography by Mark Leigh and Philippa Hatton-Lepine

Wannabe a  girl?

The Authors

Little is known about Mark Leigh and Mike Lepine except to say that they're prolific bestselling authors and that Mike fancies Posh Spice 'something rotten', while Mark fantasises about being alone with Geri, a bottle of baby oil and a sable glove.

Other books by the same sad men:

THE COMPLETE REVENGE KIT

HOW TO BE A COMPLETE BASTARD [with Adrian Edmondson]

HOW TO BE A COMPLETE BITCH [with Pamela Stephenson]

THE BOOK OF REVELATIONS

THE NAUGHTY '90s

THE RETURN OF THE COMPLETE REVENGE KIT

HOW TO BE A SUPERHERO

THE BOOK OF STUPID LISTS

HOW TO BE A REAL MAN [with Julian Clary]

THE OFFICIAL POLITICALLY INCORRECT HANDBOOK – Volume 1

BACK TO BASICS

THE ULTIMATE REVENGE KIT

ROY CHUBBY BROWN UNZIPPED! [with Roy Chubby Brown]

THE OFFICE REVENGE KIT

THE OFFICIAL POLITICALLY INCORRECT HANDBOOK – Volume 2

ANIMAL TALES [with Rolf Harris]

THE EXTRA-TERRESTRIAL'S GUIDE TO THE X-FILES

BEASTLY BEHAVIOUR [with Rolf Harris]

THE LOVERS' REVENGE KIT

Acknowledgements

A big shout goin' out to all the vibey gang who helped with this totally happenin' book!

Peter Bennett (Free Place To Stay When You Need To Write A Book Spice).

John Choopani (Run up his Phone Bill Spice).

Stephen Choopani (Mac Spice).

Amy Hart (The Other Baby Spice).

Graham & Suzanne Hart (Parents of Amy Spice).

Andrea Henry (Editor Spice).

Sophie Howell (Niece Spice)

Val Hudson (Publisher Spice).

Adam Leigh (Big Beefy Guy On The Cover Spice).

Judy Martin (Agent Spice).

Philippa Hatton-Lepine (Mike's Wife Spice).

Debbie Leigh (Mark's Wife Spice).

Polly Leigh (Real Spice Girls' Fan Spice).

Barney Leigh (Who Also Likes The Group Even Though He's Four And A Boy Spice).

and Louisa Shaw (Almost Forgot to Put Back her Bon Jovi Screensaver Spice)

P.S. Polly, Daddy's really, really sorry for saying these things about your fave group.

How to read...

What you are now looking at is called a 'page'. There are 96 of them in this book. Two pages make a 'spread'

When you have completed the right hand page, use your fingers to move it from right to left, exposing the next two pages for your reading pleasure.

Continue at your own pace until you have reached the last page, then put this book somewhere until it is time for the next car boot sale....➤

ON EACH 'SPREAD', START READING ON THE LEFT HAND SIDE

...this book!

If you find you are suffering any side effects from reading, you should put the book down and play a CD or watch TV instead.

WARNING

Friends may treat you differently if they learn that you have read a book. You may be teased, snubbed or kicked severely in the head and body and end up in intensive care. HarperCollins*Publishers* accepts no responsibility for prevailing social trends.

Introduction

'If we can do it, so can you!'

So you really, really wannabe a Spice Girl?

🖤 *Then this is the book for you!*

🖤 *And if you only read one book in your life time – then you're probably an ideal candidate for the group!*

🖤 *Here's the secret. Here's what makes the Spice Girls different.*

anyone can be a SPICE GIRL

It doesn't matter who you are, so long as you've got the VIBE you can join, and the SPICE GIRLS will WELCOME you with OPEN ARMS – warts and all. Well, obviously not if you've got warts. Big horrible facial ones with tufts of hair sticking out of them.

But provided you've got the VIBE and no warts and – well obviously – you can SING and DANCE to professional standards – ANYONE can be a SPICE GIRL!

Now's your big chance!

Anyone FEMALE, that is, but that goes without saying. After all, we are talking about the SPICE GIRLS – and not the Spice Boys.

Live the life!

You can be black or white, fat or thin (well, not fat, obviously. None of the Spice Girls are fat.) Young or old (well, not old). Pretty or plain (except for plain). Extrovert, introvert (well, not introvert. The other girls would eat you alive). IT DOESN'T MATTER!

There you have it – provided you're FEMALE, YOUNG, THIN, TALENTED, EXTROVERT and ATTRACTIVE – and can SING and DANCE, ANYONE can be a SPICE GIRL.

Make the money!

Dream THE Dream!

And we'll teach you how so that, when your big opportunity comes, you'll be ready to join THE GREATEST POP SENSATIONS of all time!

How did such a vibing group get started?

EVERYWHERE YOU LOOK, THERE SEEMS TO BE A DIFFERENT ACCOUNT OF HOW THE SPICE GIRLS GOT STARTED. STRANGE. THEIR MYSTERIOUS

THEY WERE ROCKETED TO EARTH WHEN THEIR HOME PLANET, SPICETON EXPLODED AND UNDER THE EARTH'S YELLOW SUN, DEVELOPED SUPER SINGING POWER, SUPER DANCING POWER, SUPER LYRIC-WRITING POWER AND, OF COURSE, GIRL POWER

THEY DEVELOPED FROM A VERY VIRULENT (AND STINKY) VIRUS GROWN IN A LABORATORY CULTURE DISH

PAST HAS BEEN SHROUDED IN GREAT, GREAT SECRECY LEADING

They are the last five survivors from a race of quite-intelligent beings that inhabited the lost continent of Atlantis

THEY GO WAY, WAY BACK TO BIBLICAL TIMES: 'ON THE SIXTH DAY, GOD CREATED MAN AND ON THE SEVENTH DAY, MAN CREATED THE SPICE GIRLS'

THEY WERE FOUND PRESERVED IN A HUGE BLOCK OF ICE BY THE BRITISH ANTARCTIC EXPEDITION AND SUBSEQUENTLY THAWED OUT AND BROUGHT BACK TO WESTERN CIVILIZATION.

They were created by a mad doctor who combined body parts from five different corpses and who brought them back to life (although he forgot to put in the brains)

TO MANY ODD RUMOURS. WE CAN REVEAL THAT THESE ARE ALL COMPLETELY UNTRUE. OK?

THEY DON'T REALLY EXIST AT ALL. WE'RE ALL VICTIMS OF MASS

HYPE!

1 Five beautiful girls bursting with fabulous raw talent answer an ad inviting them to audition for a new all-female group. Luckily for Geri, Victoria, Emma and the two Mels, the five girls in question go to the wrong address – leaving the stage clear for our fab five to pass the audition instead! Now comes the hard task of finding a name and an image for the band...

2 The management suggest the 'Naked Girls'. The first single 'Jump Up and Down Vigorously' is planned for September, followed by their debut album 'Oiled and Handcuffed' in time for Christmas. After much consideration, the girls feel that they are perhaps being exploited slightly and decide to leave their management.

3 Career crisis! With no management, and no record deal, the girls seek a new direction. They decide that there's no market for girl groups and decide to become a boy band instead. Two favour just dressing up in boy's clothes, while another two want to be more realistic and suggest the use of false beards and medical prosthetic appendages. One suggests a full sex change and is gossiped about forever after. The idea is eventually abandoned in favour of remaining a girl group.

4 The girls gather in a restaurant to discuss their name. For reasons never fully disclosed, they decide on a theme of food additives. The Spice Girls, suggested by Geri, is their runaway favourite name. The Herb Girls is a popular second. The E-Number Girls, the MSG Girls and the Artificial Flavourings Girls are all rejected, as is the Salmonella Girls and the Chef's Bogeys Girls.

5 Having decided on the group's name, the gals now decide they should each have a 'gang' nickname.

6 The girls come up with the idea of nicknaming themselves after their bodily ailments. 'Verruca' Spice and 'Scabby Knee' Spice are enthusiastic. 'Cellulite' Spice and 'Haemorrhoid' Spice are not. The casting vote goes to 'Thrush' Spice...

7 The girls decide instead to give each other nicknames. 'Spoiled Cow' Spice ignores the whole thing. 'Cat's Arse Face' Spice threatens to leave the band. 'Brain Dead' Spice is confused. The issue is settled amicably by lots of shouting and hair-pulling, followed by a vote at which it is agreed that the Spices can choose their own nicknames...

STILL, HERE'S THE TRUE VIBEY VERSION, TO THE BEST OF OUR KNOWLEDGE. IT COMES STRAIGHT FROM A FRIEND OF THE BROTHER OF SOMEONE WHO USED TO GO OUT WITH ONE OF THE SPICES ● SO HE SHOULD KNOW.

AND IT'S AT LEAST AS RELIABLE AS THE OFFICIAL VERSION...

Someone suggests only ever doing songs about ripe cheeses. Someone suggests only ever appearing on stage in

Now all the group needs is a gimmick!

costumes made from live Brazilian killer bees. None of the gimmicks suggested strike a chord. Geri is told to keep her ideas to herself. There is despondency. Then – a break-through! Mel C suggests feminism. The room goes quiet. Emma frantically looks it up in a dictionary. And the rest is history!

SOMEONE SUGGESTS APPEARING WITH ONIONS IN THEIR CLEAVAGES.

The origins of 'Girl Power!'

How different things might have been if the girls had gone with one of their earlier catchphrases instead of the now-classic 'Girl Power!' All the ones below were considered – and rejected...

- Show us yer nuts!
- Buy our records!
- Get your kit off, George Clooney!
- Give us yer money!
- Eternal are crap!
- We'll do anything to get a boyfriend!

After Mel C suggested Feminism as the group's gimmick, the hunt was on to find a suitable slogan to sum up the girls' deepest feelings and to copyright and put on T-shirts, sweatshirts, tote bags and any other form of lucrative merchandise available. All the slogans below were dismissed before someone hit on the 'Girl Power!' line...

- Feminine Energy!
- Ladylike Turbines!
- Girlie Gas!
- Totty Electricity!
- Lassie Power!
- Female Juice!

Without any help at all whatsoever from image consultants, pluggers, choreographers, designers, songwriters, producers, sound engineers, managers, marketing specialists, spin doctors or anyone else at all, honestly, the Spice Girls go on to become the biggest pop sensation the world has ever known!

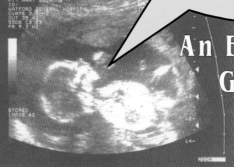

Am I too young to be a Spice Girl?

An Ex-Spice Girl Speaks!

'Any girl can get the Spice Vibe – even if you're a foetus like me. I haven't even been born but I've been Kickin' since I was a few weeks old (albeit in amniotic fluid, which might not count). The future's female and so am I, if my last scan was anything to go by.'

– Almost Full Term Spice

The future is female: #1

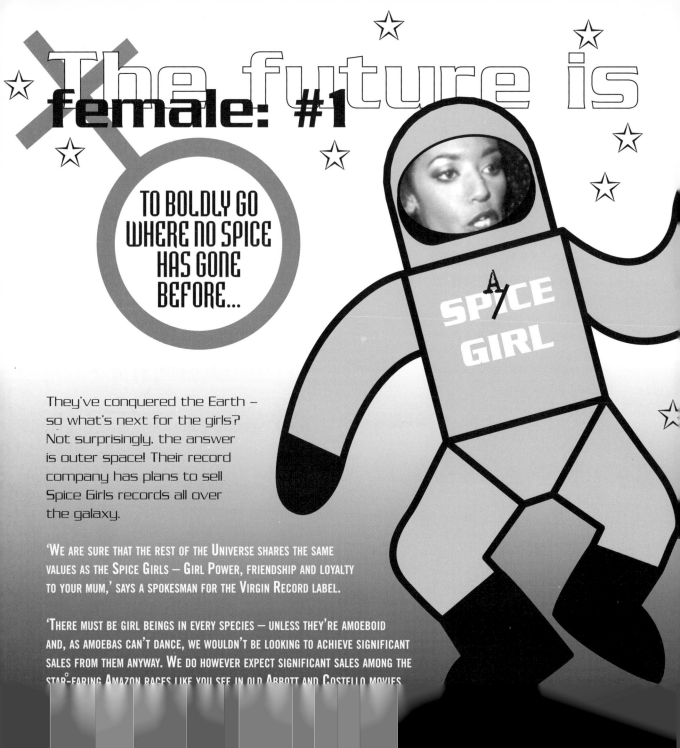

TO BOLDLY GO WHERE NO SPICE HAS GONE BEFORE...

SPICE GIRL

They've conquered the Earth – so what's next for the girls? Not surprisingly, the answer is outer space! Their record company has plans to sell Spice Girls records all over the galaxy.

'WE ARE SURE THAT THE REST OF THE UNIVERSE SHARES THE SAME VALUES AS THE SPICE GIRLS — GIRL POWER, FRIENDSHIP AND LOYALTY TO YOUR MUM,' SAYS A SPOKESMAN FOR THE VIRGIN RECORD LABEL.

'THERE MUST BE GIRL BEINGS IN EVERY SPECIES — UNLESS THEY'RE AMOEBOID AND, AS AMOEBAS CAN'T DANCE, WE WOULDN'T BE LOOKING TO ACHIEVE SIGNIFICANT SALES FROM THEM ANYWAY. WE DO HOWEVER EXPECT SIGNIFICANT SALES AMONG THE STAR-FARING AMAZON RACES LIKE YOU SEE IN OLD ABBOTT AND COSTELLO MOVIES.

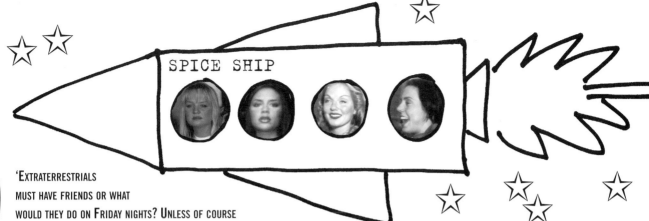

SPICE SHIP

'EXTRATERRESTRIALS MUST HAVE FRIENDS OR WHAT WOULD THEY DO ON FRIDAY NIGHTS? UNLESS OF COURSE ONE OF THEIR PLANETARY DAYS IS EQUAL TO 175 OF OUR EARTH YEARS IN WHICH CASE YOU COULD DIE WITHOUT EVER REACHING THE WEEKEND. THESE PLANETS WOULD BE UNCOOL AND WE WOULD ANTICIPATE A HARD SELL.

'ALIENS MUST HAVE MUMS TOO — UNLESS THEY'RE CLONES OR BROOD-ZYGOTES OR REPRODUCE ASEXUALLY OR IN SOME ICKY WAY THAT INVOLVES TWO MALES AND WE DON'T WANT THEM AS FANS ANYWAY.'

BUT DON'T WORRY, THE SPICE GIRLS WON'T BE LEAVING THE PLANET JUST YET.

'AT FIRST, WE WILL BE BROADCASTING SPICE GIRLS MUSIC THROUGH GIANT RADIO TELESCOPES AND TRYING TO SET UP A "PAY AS YOU LISTEN" SERVICE WITH OTHER PLANETS. THEN, AS SCIENCE PROGRESSES, WE PLAN TO FREEZE THE SPICE GIRLS AND SEND THEM IN THEIR CONTRACTUALLY OBLIGATED "CRYOGENIC SUSPENSION TOUR AROUND THE STARS".'

THERE IS ONE PROVISO IN VIRGIN'S AMBITIOUS PLANS: 'WE HOPE THAT THEY HAVE MONEY IN OUTER SPACE,' SAYS THE VIRGIN RECORDS SPOKESMAN. 'OTHERWISE THEY CAN BOG OFF.'

Spice Merchandise!

The Future is Female!

But Emma says the future in sewage treatment is the new, economical Spice Girls Decompositron XL78 Septic Tank.

IT'S CRAP!

'Having a Spice Girls Septic Tank made me the most popular girl at school!'
– MICHELLE, ST IVES

'It smells as good as it looks!'
– Tracy Bolton

Which Spice should I be?

Anyone who wants to be a Spice Girl first has to have a good Spice name. Of course, you can't just choose any old name – it's got to sound hot and not undermine the whole Girl Power vibe.

WHAT DO YOU MEAN?

Well, you couldn't very well call yourself, 'Soppy Girlie Spice', or 'What Would You Like For Your Dinner Dear?, Spice' could you?

'SPOSE NOT.

Equally, you couldn't really call yourself 'Posh Spice' if Victoria was still in the group, otherwise there would be two girls called Posh Spice and the fans would find it confusing.

BUT IF I WANTED TO CALL MYSELF POSH SPICE AS WELL, VICTORIA COULD CALL HERSELF 'THE ORIGINAL POSH SPICE' AND I COULD CALL MYSELF 'POSH SPICE 2', OR SOMETHING LIKE THAT...?

No.

OK. HOW ABOUT 'NEW POSH SPICE'?

No.

ALL RIGHT THEN. WHAT ABOUT, 'POSH SPICE – THE NEXT GENERATION'?

No! Look. There are hundreds and hundreds of names you could choose from to reflect your personality without copying one of the other Girls or having a name and image that doesn't respect Girl Power. To save you the trouble of thinking about it, here's a handy guide.

THE FUTURE IS FEMALE: #2

CYBORG SPICE WARS!

There is a possibility that, at some point in the future, in order to save the Earth, the Spice Girls' brains will have to be removed and implanted inside giant, death-dealing battle robots – but the possibility is so remote that we're not going to discuss it any further.

If I want to join the Spice Girls, is it an advantage to have spunk and balls? METAPHORICALLY SPEAKING, YES. PHYSIOLOGICALLY SPEAKING, NO.

14

YOUR IMAGE	YOUR SPICE GIRLS NAME
Someone who's really, really wild	Mental Spice
Someone who's unicellular	Amoeba Spice
Someone who's just got married	Spliced Spice
Someone who's quite pleasant	Nice Spice
Someone who likes playing board games	Dice Spice
Someone who's a Siamese Twin	Twice Spice
Someone who's the Son of God	Christ Spice
Someone with a big bust	Silicon Spice
Someone who sells their body	Vice Spice
Someone who's head of the Roman Catholic Church	Pope Spice
Someone with an itchy scalp	Lice Spice
Someone who's dyslexic	Ghdyujkuas Spice
Someone who doesn't want anyone knowing her name	
Someone who can't think of an imaginative name	Spice Spice

Do I Have To Be Able To Sing To Be A **Spice** Girl?

AN EX-SPICE GIRL SPEAKS!

'Before I joined the Spice Girls I was a model and professional singer and dancer. I was also a competent musician with a degree in poetry and prose, which proved invaluable in writing lyrics. I also studied fashion design for five years. They fired me for "not fitting in".'

'Too Smart For Her Own Good' Spice

Who were the original Spice Girls?

It's hard to believe that there could ever have been anyone like the Spice Girls before. But there was!

The Suffragettes are now only remembered for promoting Girl Power in the form of women's emancipation. Their unique musical vibe is now largely forgotten, just as H. G. Wells – the Peter Andre of Victorian England – is better known as the author of *The Time Machine* and *War of the Worlds*, rather than for his chart-topping form and oiled physique.

The Suffragettes were the original Girl Band and were just as fab in their day as the Spices are in ours!

THE EMPIRE'S PREMIER POP PERIODICAL. GOD SAVE THE KING!

SMASHING HITS

¼d AUGUST 17TH 1913

GREAT SUFFRAGETTE GIRL COMPO INSIDE! 50 WAX CYLINDERS TO BE WON!

HUNKY HERB ASQUITH
PLANET SIZE POSTER INSIDE!

THE FABIANS! WHICH ONE'S YOUR FAVE?

HOW TO DRESS LIKE SIR THOMAS BEECHAM

KAISER WILHELM - TO TOUR NEXT YEAR?

CHRISTIAN TEMPERANCE MOVEMENT - ALL THE LYRICS!

WRIGHT BROTHERS TO SPLIT? WILBUR TO FLY SOLO?

SIR EDWARD ELGAR - HOT HAIR TIPS

EXCLUSIVE!
RANKIN' LORD KITCHENER - RESPECT IS DUE!

LABOUR PARTY
NEW KIDS ON THE BLOCK!

OFFICIAL SUFFRAGETTE GIRLS MERCHANDISE OFFICIAL

A MOST IMPORTANT WARNING TO YOU, THE POTENTIAL PURCHASER!

BEFORE YOU DIVEST YOURSELF OF YOUR EARNINGS PLEASE BE ADVISED THAT IF IT DOES NOT SAY 'OFFICIAL SUFFRAGETTE GIRLS MERCHANDISE' THEN IT IS NOT. FAILURE TO HEED THIS WARNING MAY RESULT IN A WORLD WAR IN WHICH MILLIONS OF MEN WILL BE KILLED AND VERY FEW WOMEN WILL BE ABLE TO FIND SUITABLE HUSBANDS.

NEW

ROCK WITH YOUR CHUMS IN THE OFFICIAL SUFFRAGETTE GIRLS GARDEN LAWN SWING!

OFFICIAL

STANDARD 'STATIONARY' VERSION £2 3s 7d. DELUXE VERSION £3 5s 9d (MOVES BACK AND FORTH IN A GENTLE RHYTHM)

HOORAH! KEEP YOUR SAVOURIES AND DELECTABLES FRESH WITH THE FRESHEST GROUP AROUND!

OFFICIAL

BARGAIN

THE OFFICIAL SUFFRAGETTE GIRLS BISCUIT TIN (80% LEAD, 20% IRON) 1s 3d

SUFFRAGETTE GIRLS PARASOL PUTS UNOFFICIAL SUFFRAGETTE PARASOLS IN THE SHADE

CHEAP

OFFICIAL

(CAN ALSO BE USED IN INCLEMENT CONDITIONS) 2s 5d

OFFICIAL SUFFRAGETTE GIRLS POSTERIOR PORTMANTEAU £4 7s 6d

OFFICIAL

SUFFRAGETTE GIRLS SAUCY BEACH WEAR!

4/- (+P&P)

PHWOAR! NOT BAD AT ALL!

The future is female: #3

OWN YOUR OWN SPICE GIRLS!!!!!

IMAGINE THAT!

Today, you couldn't possibly have enough money to own a top-earning act like the Spice Girls but – thanks to cloning technology – the price could soon tumble!

Today, it's only possible to clone sheep – and they can't sing – but if science keeps advancing, it may soon be possible to clone Spice Girls at pocket money prices! We've already seen this with Boy Bands.

Instead of listening to a CD, your Spice Girls could perform live for you in your very own living room. You could decide what they sing, what they do, what they wear and what they say. It's just like being Virgin Records!

just how big are the Spice Girls?

It's official! The Spice Girls have conquered the world! Girl Power has swept the globe and there's just no stopping it!

They've achieved what even previous Top World Conquering Act Adolf Hitler couldn't do – even though he bore an uncanny resemblance to our favourite popsters! He could shout like Mel B, be as surly as Victoria or as childish as Emma, high kick the goose step like Mel C, and was as nutty, short and flatulent as Geri.

Despite this he never got it together with the same sort of success. If only he'd had a grooving vibe, great tunes and better legs, maybe things would have been different, but for now the Spice Girls are on top!

Just see how the Spice Girls compare with these other second-rate world-beaters!

THE PHOENICIAN EMPIRE
1200–332 BC

THE SEAFARING PHOENICIANS MAY HAVE DOMINATED THE MEDITERRANEAN FROM SYRIA AND THE LEBANON THROUGH TO CARTHAGE AND EVEN SAILED TO BRITAIN, BUT THEY'RE CERTAINLY OCEANS APART FROM THE SPICE GIRLS WHEN IT COMES TO MAKING WAVES IN THE POP BIZ! MAYBE THAT'S WHY THEY WERE ALL WASHED UP BY 332BC!

HOW DO THEY COMPARE?

Had their own fan club. – NO

Choreographed their own dance routines. – NO

Invited to switch on the Christmas lights in Oxford Street. – NO

Posed topless. – NO

THE BRITISH EMPIRE
1607–1945

BRITAIN'S PREVIOUS GREATEST ACHIEVEMENT BEFORE THE SPICE GIRLS. RESPONSIBLE FOR MANY DREADFUL ACTS LIKE SPREADING CRICKET THROUGHOUT THE WORLD. IT PLUNDERED JEWELS AND MINERAL WEALTH FROM HALF THE WORLD FOR OVER THREE CENTURIES – BUT STILL DIDN'T MAKE AS MUCH MONEY AS THE SPICE GIRLS' FIRST SINGLE.

HOW DO THEY COMPARE?

Won the hearts of Americans rather than being unceremoniously chucked out by them in 1776. – NO

Stood for peace and love rather than hitting brown people with long sticks. – NO

Had a US chart Top 5 Album smash sensation. – NO

Sponsored by Pepsi. – NO

THE HABSBURG EMPIRE
1867–1918

THE KAJAGOOGOO OF THE EMPIRE WORLD – NOW LONG FORGOTTEN AND NOT PARTICULARLY SIGNIFICANT AT THE TIME, EITHER. THAT'S ABOUT IT, REALLY.

HOW DO THEY COMPARE?

EVER ASKED TO STAR IN A COMIC RELIEF SPECTACULAR. – NO

LEFT US ANY SONGS AS GOOD AS '2 BECOME 1'? – NO

WON THE SUN'S BIZARRE READERS' POLL. – NO

HAD A FOOD FIGHT WITH RIGHT SAID FRED. – NO [HAD MORE SERIOUS FIGHT WITH LESS TRENDY OTTOMANS INSTEAD]

THE AZTEC EMPIRE
1200–1519

A THEOCRATIC STATE, THE AZTEC EMPIRE WAS FOUNDED ON HUMAN SACRIFICE. THEY NEVER INVENTED THE WHEEL SO WERE UNABLE TO MAKE THE NEXT EVOLUTIONARY STEP UP TO THE DJ'S TURNTABLE. THEIR SOLE CONTRIBUTION TO WORLD MUSIC WAS THE NOSE FLUTE WHICH IS IMPOSSIBLE TO DANCE TO. THEY MAY HAVE HAD EL DORADO – THE LEGENDARY 'CITY OF GOLD' – BUT YOU CAN BET THEY HAD NO GOLD DISCS!

HOW DO THEY COMPARE?

Broke every record for an all-girl band. – NO

Had tea with Courtney Love. – NO

Won a coveted Brit Award. – NO

Pulled its bikini bottom down to prove to a journalist that it was not a natural red head. – NO

Looked as good in a halter top as Geri. – HARDLY

Dated top Liverpool football player. – PROBABLY NOT

THE MONGOL EMPIRE
1206–1405 AD

LED BY GENGHIS KHAN – THE SCARY SPICE OF HIS DAY – THE MONGOL HORDES CARVED OUT AN EMPIRE FROM GERMANY TO KOREA, BUT NEVER HAD A HIT RECORD IN TWO CENTURIES. WHICH JUST GOES TO PROVE WHAT A VERY SPECIAL TALENT THE SPICE GIRLS HAVE!

HOW DO THEY COMPARE?

Number of Albums to reach Number 1 in the UK. – 0

Shouted 'Show us your tits!' at Kula Shaker. – NO

Had less manners than the Spice Girls. – The Jury is still out

Good to their mums. – Not especially

THE ROMAN EMPIRE
753BC–410 AD

THEY SAY THAT ALL ROADS LEAD TO ROME, BUT FOR THE SPICE GIRLS, ALL ROADS THESE DAYS SEEM TO LEAD TO THE TOP OF THE CHARTS! ROME CLAIMED TO BE A BASTION OF CIVILIZATION BUT HAD NO HIT PARADE SO IT WAS HARDLY AN ADVANCED CULTURE! PRODUCED NO ACTS OF THE CALIBRE OF THE SPICE GIRLS. THE BIGGEST BOX OFFICE DRAW AT THE COLISEUM WAS A LARGE LION CALLED MR HUNGRY. SO IT'S THUMBS UP FOR THE SPICE GIRLS AND THUMBS DOWN FOR ROMAN CIVILIZATION!

HOW DO THEY COMPARE?

Number of consecutive singles straight in at Number 1. – 0

Conquered the known world through sheer vibe-osity rather than force of arms. – NO

Made boring things like aquaducts, forums and straight roads rather than mini-masterpieces of pop. – YES

Descended into barbarism and collapsed rather than consolidating its grip on the pop charts. – YES

So you think
you know the Spice Girls?

Do you really know the Spice Girls?

Well here's one way to find out – in this Rappin' Spices Quiz!

Do you really, really know the Spice Girls?

We all know the Girls love to mouth off about anyone and anything but what's important is that they say what they mean. Not only that, they mean what they say. They also say mean what they – except when they're doing this, no one understands what they're on about.

To see if you share the same vibe as the Spice Girls, try and match the five real quotes on this page with the five Girls who said them. It doesn't matter if you don't know – just go for the answer you think is right. Remember, believe in yourself!

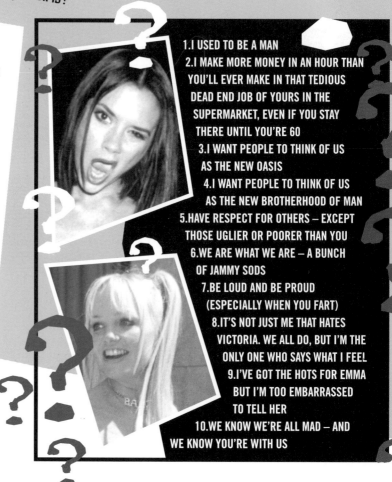

1. I USED TO BE A MAN
2. I MAKE MORE MONEY IN AN HOUR THAN YOU'LL EVER MAKE IN THAT TEDIOUS DEAD END JOB OF YOURS IN THE SUPERMARKET, EVEN IF YOU STAY THERE UNTIL YOU'RE 60
3. I WANT PEOPLE TO THINK OF US AS THE NEW OASIS
4. I WANT PEOPLE TO THINK OF US AS THE NEW BROTHERHOOD OF MAN
5. HAVE RESPECT FOR OTHERS – EXCEPT THOSE UGLIER OR POORER THAN YOU
6. WE ARE WHAT WE ARE – A BUNCH OF JAMMY SODS
7. BE LOUD AND BE PROUD (ESPECIALLY WHEN YOU FART)
8. IT'S NOT JUST ME THAT HATES VICTORIA. WE ALL DO, BUT I'M THE ONLY ONE WHO SAYS WHAT I FEEL
9. I'VE GOT THE HOTS FOR EMMA BUT I'M TOO EMBARRASSED TO TELL HER
10. WE KNOW WE'RE ALL MAD – AND WE KNOW YOU'RE WITH US

The Spice Girls are human • just like you and me. They just have more money, that's all.

11. I LIKE SLEDGE-HAMMERING SMALL MAMMALS
12. STICK WITH YOUR MATES, WELL, UNTIL YOU GET BORED, THEN DUMP 'EM
13. TAKE CONTROL OF YOUR LIFE!
14. TAKE CONTROL OF YOUR BLADDER!
15. I WAS ENGAGED, BUT BROKE AWAY AND FOUND MYSELF AND MY FRIENDS WHEN I REALIZED HE WASN'T RIGHT FOR ME
16. WE'RE SUCH CRAP
17. WE ARE WHAT WE ARE – CAREFULLY PACKAGED, ARTIFICIALLY MANUFACTURED HYPE
18. STAND UP FOR WHAT YOU BELIEVE IN, PROVIDING IT'S NOT GOING TO MAKE YOU UNPOPULAR
19. NO ONE'S GONNA CHANGE THE WAY WE LOOK, FEEL OR THINK (UNLESS THEY OFFER US A SHITLOAD OF MONEY FIRST)
20. EVERY TIME EMMA SINGS OFF KEY I SLAP HER. I'VE GOT A VERY SORE HAND
21. SHE'S NOT POSH AT ALL. I SAW HER PICK HER NOSE AND EAT IT
22. I'M A VIRGIN
23. I TRY AND MAKE THE MOST OF WHAT I'VE GOT – EVEN IF I AM A SMALL GINGER RUNT
24. I TRY AND MAKE THE BEST OF WHAT I'VE GOT – EVEN IF I'M SMALL, I THINK TALL
25. I'M GAGGING FOR IT
26. I FEEL LIKE A MAN TRAPPED IN A GIRL'S BODY
27. IF YOU WANT TO STAND UP AND SAY, 'AAAARGH!' THEN DO IT
28. IF YOU WANT TO STAND UP AND RUN OUT OF OUR CONCERTS SAYING, 'I WANT MY MONEY BACK!', THEN DO IT
29. MY DAD IS KEITH HARRIS – OF KEITH HARRIS AND ORVILLE FAME

Answers

MEL C: 3
EMMA: 10
VICTORIA: 15
GERI: 24
MEL B: 27

How Can I Be Like - POSH SPICE ?

BUUUURP!

- Smouldering Latin brown eyes are so sexy (try wearing sunglasses if you've got boring eyes. Or consider corneal grafts!)
- A Teri Hatcher hand-me-down haircut can look extra cool!
- Slim, sleek body (try going on a harsh diet)
- Wear expensive designer clothes! (Try winning them in a competition if you're poor)
- Great Tan (it comes from the Spanish in her. If you'd like some Spanish in you, try chatting up the waiters on holiday)

GET THE LOOK! #1

- Rigid body posture (try clenching your buttocks and go from there)
- Pout like you've got the world's worst case of constipation!
- Glare like your little sister has just appeared in your best outfit — with a jam sandwich in her hands (and you've got super PMT and it's Monday morning)

HOW TO BE ENIGMATIC AND SOPHISTICATED LIKE POSH SPICE

1. Don't say anything
2. Don't do anything

HOW TO HAVE ATTITUDE!

IF THERE'S ONE THING VICTORIA'S GOT — ASIDE FROM OODLES AND OODLES OF DOSH — IT'S ATTITUDE. WHAT IS ATTITUDE? WELL, BACK IN YOUR PARENTS' DAYS THEY USED TO CALL IT RUDENESS OR ARROGANCE, BUT THEN THEY USED TO DANCE TO DURAN DURAN ALBUMS. THIS IS THE 1990S AND THINGS HAVE CHANGED!

- Don't reply when people talk to you
- Glare at complete strangers like they were made of pure snot
- Only nerds say 'please', 'thank you' or ask permission
- Never show any gratitude. Look upon any favour or gift like someone just spat loads on your favourite T-shirt.
- Don't use two words when one will do (or one word when a supercilious sneer or offhand grunt will suffice)
- Master the art of looking bored. It pays!
- Smoke where you know you shouldn't – like around babies and in octane-rich environments

HOW NOT TO SMILE

VICTORIA HATES SMILING.

IF YOU WANT TO AVOID SMILING, HERE ARE SOME THINGS TO THINK ABOUT:
- YOUR GRANDAD'S BOTTOM
- YOUR JOB
- YOUR LIFE
- WHAT YOU WEIGH
- HOW YOU'RE GOING TO DIE
- DOUBLE MATHS ON MONDAY MORNING
- WHAT HAPPENED DURING THOSE FIFTEEN MINUTES WHEN YOUR BOYFRIEND AND YOUR BEST MATE BOTH WENT MISSING FROM YOUR XMAS PARTY
- YOUR CHANCES OF EVER GETTING IN THE SPICE GIRLS

DON'T THINK ABOUT:
- CUDDLY KITTENS
- THE FUNNIEST JOKE YOU EVER HEARD
- YOUR BOYFRIEND PROPOSING
- THE PINK POWER RANGER (WHO YOUR BOYFRIEND FANCIES) ACCIDENTLY CATCHING ON FIRE

VICTORIA HAS...

- CLASS
- POISE
- ATTITUDE
- A HORNY FIANCEE
- PROBLEMS GETTING ON WITH PEOPLE
- A SURPRISINGLY COMMON ACCENT
- A DEEP SENSE OF IRONY WHEN IT CAME TO CHOOSING HER SPICE NAME
- LOTS OF MONEY

Who invented Girl Power?

If you wannabe a Spice Girl you need to understand the origins of Girl Power, and the best way to do this is by learning about it from history.

Now the first girl to have Girl Power was Eve. You know, as in Adam and Eve. She wasn't just the first woman, she was the first ever Spice Girl! Now we don't mean she was in a totally happening girl band – because there weren't any other girls at that time. Or bands. Not even Status Quo. No, what we mean is that she had the independence vibe from the word go. She wore what she wanted (to start with, nothing) and she wasn't going to let anyone tell her how to live her life – not even God! This is her story. Read it loud and proud.

1. Then the Lord made woman. And she was called Eve Spice and she had a totally cool vibe and was dead laid back.

2. And Adam and Eve were both naked but they felt no shame. Wicked!

3. And they were free to do as they pleased in the Garden of Eden. Except for one thing. God forbade them to eat from the Tree of Life because he was a real control freak.

4. But Eve was in control of her own life and no omnipotent, omnipresent, omniscient supreme male being was gonna tell her what to do.

5. Now Eve had a mate called Serpent Spice who was absolutely Kicking! He told Eve that it was OK to eat the forbidden fruit. So she did and it was a dead tasty vibe.

GIRL POWER

6. And after Eve Spice had eaten the forbidden fruit she became aware of her nakedness and wanted to make a fashion statement. But there were no designer labels in those days. So she did the best she could with three fig leaves.

7. But the Lord appeared and said to her, 'Why did you eat the forbidden fruit?' and Eve Spice replied, 'The Serpent said it would be a good laugh and I stick with my mates! Now get off my case, you're doin' my head in!'

8. But the Lord got psyched up about her attitude and banished Eve Spice, Serpent Spice and Adam East of Eden. But as Eden didn't have any shops or places to do lunch, it was hardly paradise.

9. And Eve Spice didn't give a monkey's what anyone thought about her because she was strong-willed and believed in herself.

10. And respect was due.

The only real difference between Eve and the Spice Girls today was that Eve didn't love her mother. Mainly because she never had one. She was actually born of Adam's rib – and a song called 'Rib' would sound dead naff:

'Rib' by Eve Spice

'Rib I love you,
Rib I care,
Rib I love you,
Rib my friend,
My friend'

Spice Merchandise!

Victoria Talking Fashion Doll! 10" of pure sophistication!

DRESS HER UP!

TAKE HER SHOPPING!

DO LUNCH!

WITH LIFE-LIKE FEET STAMPING SULKING ACTION!

JUST IMAGINE THE FUN YOU'D HAVE WITH YOUR VICTORIA TALKING FASHION DOLL! SHOPPING AT THE RIGHT SHOPS. DINING AT THE RIGHT PLACES. MEETING THE RIGHT PEOPLE. THINGS THAT YOU'D NEVER EVER DO IN REAL LIFE IN A MILLION, BILLION YEARS!

(N.B. DRESSING YOUR VICTORIA TALKING FASHION DOLL UP IN BARBI OR CINDY CLOTHES IS ILLEGAL AND COULD LEAD TO PROSECUTION, NO MATTER HOW YOUNG YOU ARE)

SAYS 10 AUTHENTIC PHRASES!

- CHARGE IT!
- DO YOU KNOW WHO YOU'RE TALKING TO?
- I COULD HAVE YOU FIRED!
- SERVE ME FIRST. I'M FAMOUS!
- I DON'T CARE WHAT IT COSTS!
- GET ME THE MANAGER!
- GET ME MR AL FAYED!
- I'LL TAKE THEM ALL!
- THAT'S NOT EXPENSIVE ENOUGH!
- IT MIGHT BE GOOD ENOUGH FOR LIZ HURLEY, BUT IT'S NOT GOOD ENOUGH FOR ME!

OFFICIAL ACCESSORIES

- HARVEY NICHOLS PLAY SET (£89)
- SAN LORENZO WINDOW SEAT DIORAMA (£95)
- STRETCHED LIMO (£69)
- NEW YORK STYLE LOFT APARTMENT (£465)
- LOUIS VUITTON WALLET AND GOLD CREDIT CARDS (£29)
- RICH ARAB (£82)
- CLOTHES TO DIE FOR – PRADA, GUCCI, PLEIN SUD, AND JEAN PAUL GAULTIER STARTER SET (£125)

BUY LOTS

Am I too plain to be a Spice Girl?

Being a Spice Girl means always being yourself and taking pride in yourself, no matter who you are or what you look like. Within reason.

We all know that the Spice Girls have got where they are on their talent, rather than their looks – but they look fab too!

The reason is that the Spices always get with the vibe, live large, straddle the Spice-O-Sphere and their own natural beauty just comes shining through.

And, if you live the Spice Life, the same could happen with you – if you've got natural beauty to come shining through in the first place.

If you haven't, there's always plastic surgery – or Eternal.

Just remember – looks aren't everything. There's also money.

GET SPICE GIRL BEAUTIFUL!

Here, the girls share their own fabulous beauty secrets with you!

MEL B

Mel B has been described as 'a raging beauty' – and who are we to argue with her mum? Mel has great looking skin. Her secret? It's just naturally that way – so that's a fat lot of use! Mel advises you always to use make-up to make yourself look more attractive rather than like some sort of drugged-out mega loser creepazoid geek. Good advice, Mel!

TOP BEAUTY TIP

Never stick your face in a deep fat fryer.

GERI

Geri thinks you should have fun with your make up. Perhaps take it out to Stringfellows or have a slumber party with it. Make-up can be your best friend, she explains. It's always there for you and it never bitches – except for Boots eyeliner. I learned that the hard way.

TOP BEAUTY TIP

Be yourself – unless you're really tragic, in which case consult a plastic surgeon.

MEL C

Mel C isn't a big fan of make-up, which explains quite a lot. She believes you can look good without make-up – but only if you look good without make-up. Thanks for the tip, Mel.

TOP BEAUTY TIP

Get lots of sleep – and try to avoid getting hit in the face by too many footballs.

VICTORIA

Victoria attributes her lack of wrinkles to the fact that she's not old and disgusting yet. She is particularly fond of plucking her eyebrows out completely and drawing them in with pencil to achieve that extra haughty look. She recommends using only the very best cosmetics and getting filthy rich so that you can afford them.

TOP BEAUTY TIP

Look like me, not the others.

EMMA

You need a lot of make-up to look young and natural, so Emma is the expert of the group, especially on foundation and powders. She advises putting lipstick on your lips and not eating it, no matter how stressed or homesick you feel or how much you miss your mum. She also advises putting eye shadow around the eyes and not into the eyes as it is less painful and easier to see.

TOP BEAUTY TIP

Wear make-up.

Should I stick with my boyfriend or should I be a 'Spice Girls single'?

'I WAS ENGAGED, ~~BU~~T BROKE AWAY AND ~~F~~OUND MYSELF AND MY FRIENDS'

Why would you possibly want to be around boys when you can hang out with Mel B, Geri and the gang? Boys are loud, rude, vulgar, uncouth, common show-offs. Who wants that? Get with your friends instead!

However, you're not in the group yet, are you, and so you still need things like Chinese meals and semi-expensive presents. Best to stick with your boyfriend until you've joined the group – then dump him like a ton of bricks.

DO SAY: ✓

It's the pressure of success

Being on the road has pushed us apart

I need time with my friends in the band

Let's cool it – but still be friends

DON'T SAY: ✗

I'm a star and you're a non-entity. Push off!

Now I'm famous I can shag soccer stars and pop icons, so who needs you?

A woman who earns as much as I do should never have to settle for a manhood like yours

FRIENDS vs BOYFRIENDS • THE ETERNAL DILEMMA

Should you be his lover? Or should you get with your friends? That's a toughie...

BOYFRIENDS

PROS

- THEY BUY YOU THINGS
- THEY TAKE YOU PLACES
- THEY PROVE YOU AREN'T GAY
  – AND THAT SOMEONE WANTS TO GO OUT WITH YOU
- THEY USUALLY HAVE CARS
- THEY UPSET YOUR PARENTS

CONS

- YOU KNOW THEY'RE JUST USING YOU
- THEY SMELL A BIT
- APPARENTLY, IF THEY WASH THEY DIE
- THEY CAN'T UNDERSTAND YOU
  – AND DON'T EVEN TRY TO
- THEY DON'T KNOW WHAT'S GOING ON IN BROOKSIDE
- THEIR IDEA OF FOREPLAY IS BUYING YOU A BAG OF CHIPS

FRIENDS

PROS

- They understand you
- They don't want you to cover them with whipped cream
- They understand what a period is and don't go all sulky and refuse to speak to you
- You can be yourself (instead of pretending to be Alicia Silverstone like your boyfriend begged you)

CONS

- You don't fancy them
- If they make you go all nice and warm and gooey something's seriously wrong
- They expect you to pay your own way
- They're no good for a snog when you're in the mood

HOW TO ATTRACT PREMIER LEAGUE SOCCER STAR BOYFRIENDS

Wow – once you've hit the big time you'll be able to date the kind of boys you really deserve – like professional soccer league players! Here's how to snare the Premier League hunk of your own at a swanky nightclub:

HOW TO ATTRACT HIS ATTENTION

- Wear something tasteless and obvious
- Drink something rainbow coloured with an umbrella in it
- Giggle loudly
- Do the splits on the dance floor
- Adjust your cleavage every six seconds or so
- Stick your tongue in his ear
- Stick your hand in his flies
- All of the above in quick succession — or simultaneously if possible

There! He's interested. Now all you have to do is reel him in.

DO

- Admire his muscles
- Pretend you haven't heard that chat up line a thousand times before
- Pretend you know which club he plays for
- Pretend you care
- Say yes within three minutes of meeting him (or you stand to lose him!)

DON'T

- Tell his mates off for pinching your bum on the way out
- Wear knickers. He hasn't been out with anyone who's worn them before and it may confuse and possibly frighten him. Ditto a bra. He might get his hand caught and panic and cause a scene in the car park
- Mention the fact that you've got GCSEs
- Ask him how many he's got
- Mention Girl Power

Which Spice Girl am I like?

Just turn the page round (in the same direction clock hands move) to find out!

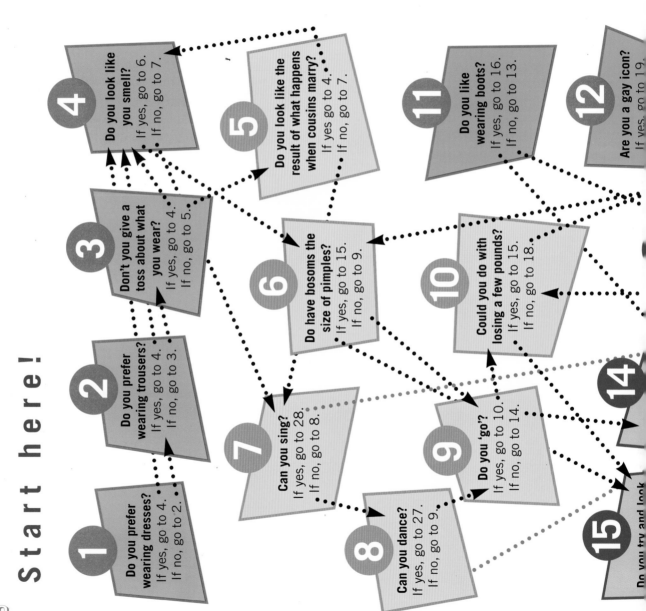

Start here!

1 Do you prefer wearing dresses? If yes, go to 4. If no, go to 2.

2 Do you prefer wearing trousers? If yes, go to 4. If no, go to 3.

3 Don't you give a toss about what you wear? If yes, go to 4. If no, go to 5.

4 Do you look like you smell? If yes, go to 6. If no, go to 7.

5 Do you look like the result of what happens when cousins marry? If yes go to 4. If no, go to 7.

6 Do have bosoms the size of pimples? If yes, go to 15. If no, go to 9.

7 Can you sing? If yes, go to 28. If no, go to 8.

8 Can you dance? If yes, go to 27. If no, go to 9.

9 Do you 'go'? If yes, go to 10. If no, go to 14.

10 Could you do with losing a few pounds? If yes, go to 15. If no, go to 18.

11 Do you like wearing boots? If yes, go to 16. If no, go to 13.

12 Are you a gay icon? If yes, go to 19.

14

15 Do you try and look

EVERYONE WHO WANTS TO BE ANYONE, WANTS TO BE A SPICE GIRL. WHILE MOST FANS CAN INSTANTLY IDENTIFY WITH AT LEAST ONE OF THE BAND, THE GIRLS ARE SO APPEALING THAT SOME WANNABES JUST CAN'T MAKE UP THEIR MINDS WHO THEY'D WANT TO BE LIKE — AND WHO COULD BLAME THEM?

IF YOU'RE CONFUSED AS TO WHO YOU MOST RESEMBLE, JUST TAKE THIS SIMPLE TEST!

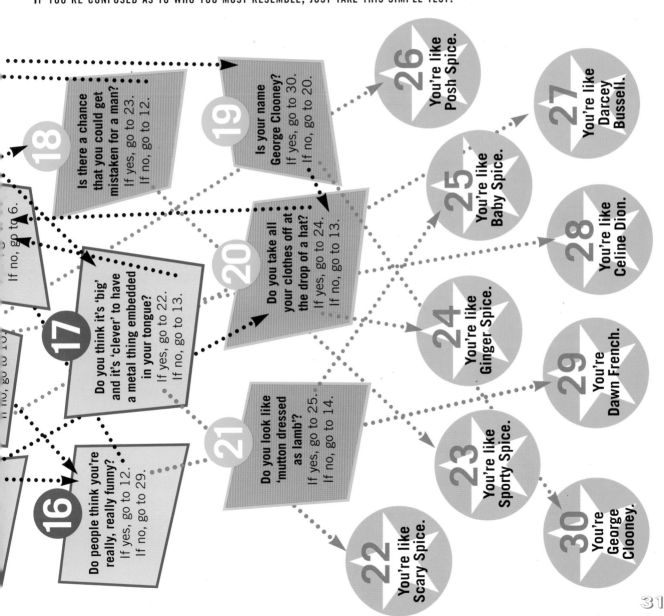

18

Is there a chance that you could get mistaken for a man?
If yes, go to 23.
If no, go to 12.

19

Is your name George Clooney?
If yes, go to 30.
If no, go to 20.

17

Do you think it's 'big' and it's 'clever' to have a metal thing embedded in your tongue?
If yes, go to 22.
If no, go to 13.

20

Do you take all your clothes off at the drop of a hat?
If yes, go to 24.
If no, go to 13.

16

Do people think you're really, really funny?
If yes, go to 12.
If no, go to 29.

21

Do you look like 'mutton dressed as lamb'?
If yes, go to 25.
If no, go to 14.

26
You're like Posh Spice.

27
You're like Darcey Bussell.

25
You're like Baby Spice.

28
You're like Celine Dion.

24
You're like Ginger Spice.

29
You're Dawn French.

23
You're like Sporty Spice.

30
You're George Clooney.

22
You're like Scary Spice.

If no, go to 6.

'Spice Spirituality'

I've heard a lot about 'Spice Spirituality'. How can I feel the healthy vibe inside?

The Spice Girls aren't just about music! They have a message too – if you're listening – and that message is all about getting in touch with yourself!

Can the Girls really tell you what you really really want deep down inside? The answer is yes – which is a relief otherwise we'd have to put a big picture of the Girls on this page to fill it up. The secret of Spice Spirituality is to indulge yourself. How better to get in touch with the 'real you' than to indulge yourself completely and discover what the 'real you' really really wants?

Who knows what you may discover if you go on a voyage of Spice Spirituality. Maybe you'll find out that you really want a sports car, or a diamond necklace! Maybe you'll even discover you want lots of money and to be famous!

THINK POSITIVE!

The Girls have developed their own meditation exercise to help them get in touch with their spiritual side. You can try it too! Just repeat the Spice Mantra again and again...

PESOS, DINARS, DOLLARS, CENTS
CRUZEIROS, SHEKELS, POUNDS AND PENCE
KENYAN SHILLINGS, RIELS AND SEN
DEUTCHMARKS, LIRA, GUILDERS, YEN
KOPEKS, ROUBLES, PUNTS, ZLOTI
SALVADORIAN COLONS, FRANCS, MALOTI
HONG KONG DOLLARS, DRACHMA, RAND
THAT IS WHY I'M IN THIS BAND

GUCCI, GAUTIER, FLASHY CAR
EXPENSIVE RESTAURANTS, CAVIAR
LOTS OF MONEY, TONS OF WEALTH
ALL TO SPEND UPON MYSELF

THE SPICE GIRLS PRAYER

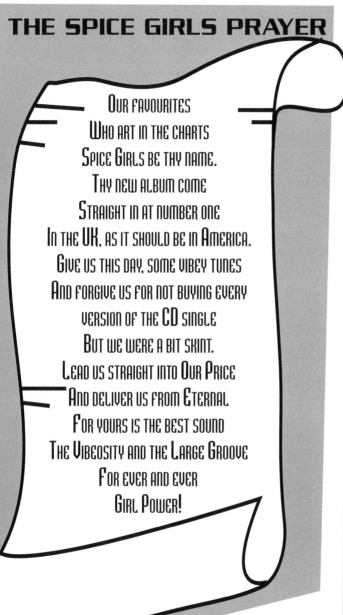

Our favourites
Who art in the charts
Spice Girls be thy name.
Thy new album come
Straight in at number one
In the UK, as it should be in America.
Give us this day, some vibey tunes
And forgive us for not buying every
version of the CD single
But we were a bit skint.
Lead us straight into Our Price
And deliver us from Eternal
For yours is the best sound
The Vibeosity and the Large Groove
For ever and ever
Girl Power!

Spice Merchandise!

Box clever – with your very own Spice Girls Empty Box!

Be the first in your class to own a Spice Girls Empty Box!

Great for parties! Guaranteed 100% empty!

If you only ever buy one empty box in your life, make sure it's this one!

'WE'RE NOT SQUARE – BUT THIS IS'*

says sexy Geri!

IT'S MADE OF CARD!

Put things in it!

Take things out of it!

Put it in the cupboard, under the stairs – 101 places!

* BOX ACTUALLY OBLONG

Trust it
Use it
Prove it
Groove it

ONLY £49.99!
PLUS P&P (SOME ASSEMBLY IS REQUIRED)

Am I too old
to be a Spice Girl?

An important part of the whole Girl Power vibe is not worrying about your appearance or the sort of person you are. However, being old does pose a few problems. Not that there's anything wrong with being old. The Spice Girls' mums are old. Some of them are even in their forties but they still lead full and active lives.

No. But if you're wondering why you haven't seen Incontinent Spice, Sholley Spice, Blue Rinse Spice, Hip Joint Spice or Alzheimer's Spice, the problem arises because life as a Spice Girl is one big party and from experience, many older Spice Girls haven't had the energy or stamina to stay the pace.

Are YOU too old to be a Spice Girl?

Try this simple quiz to find out!

When you see someone with a nose ring what do you think?
A) What's a nose ring?
B) Don't cows and pigs have those sort of things?
C) It's not as good as mine.

What would you buy with a spare £150?
A) The biggest, brashest tattoo I could afford.
B) I'd have a weekend in Broadstairs and send ten shillings to my grandson in Australia.
C) A tin of cat food (and save the rest for a rainy day).

Do you remember where you were when Elvis died?
A) Elvis who?
B) He's dead, so he's irrelevant.
C) At my Golden Wedding anniversary.

What was the first record you ever bought?
A) We didn't have records when I was young. We saved up our pennies to hear Al Bowley at the Golders Green Hippodrome. Ah, they were the days.
B) 'Mama' by the Spice Girls.
C) 'Mammy' by Al Jolson.

Do you worry about dying young?
A) No. I want to go out in a blaze of glory like Kurt Cobain!

B) No. It's far too late for that. When you get to my age blah blah blah blah...
C) I used to, during the Zeppelin raids.

Do you wish every night was Saturday night?
A) Yes. Because it means I can watch Stars In Their Eyes with that delightful Mr Matthew Kelly.
B) No. Because Thursday's the day I get my pension.
C) Yes. I can hang out, dance, get drunk and snog. Brill!

What's your biggest fear?
A) My tattoo going septic.
B) Stepping off the pavement.
C) Who'll look after 'Tiddles' when I'm gone?

Who's your pin up?
A) George Formby.
B) George Bernard Shaw.
C) George Clooney. He's got such a tasty bum!

What's your definition of the 'Good Old Days'?
A) The street party to celebrate King George's coronation.
B) When you used to get Star Wars Tazos in Walkers Crisps.
C) When you could buy a bag of broken biscuits for a tuppeny farthing.

What clubs do you belong to?
A) The Womens Institute.
B) The Ministry of Sound.
C) The RAC (well, I daren't take chances any more with my Austin Cambridge).

What does 150 beats per minute mean to you?
A) My pulse after I've taken one of those dodgy pills at a rave club.
B) My pulse when I'm pushing my Sholley.
C) The optimum way to make a soufflé when your children come round on Mothering Sunday.

What words best describe the Spice Girls?
A) Dirty little minxes!
B) Wild and Kicking!
C) I think they're great. That Bea Arthur really makes me laugh and as for Estelle Getty blah blah blah blah...

What's the worst thing ever to happen to you?
A) Catching TB.
B) Hearing that my late husband had been killed in his Spitfire over the Weald of Kent.
C) Hearing that Take That had split up.

Score:
If you care about your score, you're too old!

An Ex-Spice Girl Speaks!

'In theory it was a good idea, letting me join the group. They said they saw me as a grandmother-figure. Well I used to be a Tiller girl in my youth and thought I could teach

these young whippersnappers a thing or two about dancing. Looking back, things started to go wrong from Day One. My artificial hip popped out of its socket when I tried to copy one of Mel C's high kicks and I was out of action for sixteen weeks. Then just when I rejoined the group my lumbago starting playing up something rotten and I was on my back for another ten and the Girls had to cancel their world tour.

'We eventually split because of "artistic differences". Well, I thought that 'If You Wannabe My Old Time Dancing Partner', 'I'm 4-Ever Blowing Bubbles', 'Down By The Old Bull And Bush' and 'If U Were The Only Boy In The World' were good ideas. That's the trouble with youth today.' **Mature Spice**

Another Ex-Spice Girl Speaks!

'With hindsight I could see that my presence in the band was doomed from the start. They got rid of me on the grounds of my age but I know the real reason they dumped me was because I was a man's aftershave, and not at all suited to singing or dancing (or anything else except being splashed on someone's face).' **Old Spice**

The future is female: #4

TOP SECRET - THE SPICE GIRLS' FUTURE MUSICAL DIRECTION!

They're going to be doing – more of the same! Keep it under your hat, Spice Fans!

How can I talk like a Spice Girl?

If you've got Girl Power the language vibe will come easy. in a totally honest, hassle-free way. Just like in this kickin' sentence. But if you need a little help spicing up your language big time, then pay respect to this course:

LingoPhone 'Let's Speak Spice'

BEFORE

'I was really very excited about going out, however my boyfriend stood me up which I found quite annoying and objectionable.'

Now **YOU** CAN RAP LIKE A **SPICE GIRL** IN LESS THAN **30** DAYS!

AFTER

'I was psyched up to the max about this whole date vibe but that dweeb was a no-show who's done my head in. But who cares!'

Learning how to SPEAK SPICE is a TOTALLY EASY VIBE! All you do is play the KICKIN' cassettes LOUD and PROUD, repeating the words and phrases and following them in your free 'TALK THE TALK' text book!

After just a few minutes your ear will become used to the WICKED rhythms and sounds of the new language. A language that's not only a FAB THANG, but one that will never, ever, ever, ever DIE! Guaranteed. These words will never sound as sad as four week old SLANG!

What's even more HAPPENIN', is that it doesn't take long to learn the complete Spice Girls VOCAB VIBE: There are only twenty words in the whole Spice Girls lexicon. And lexicon isn't one of them!

What's more, as Geri and the gang think up BRILL new words, we'll rush them to you for NO EXTRA DOSH, while they're still RED HOT and STRETCHING THE VOCAB. ENVELOPE!

After your first lesson, SPEAKING SPICE will be as natural as breaking wind on top of a crowded bus on the way home from school.

Don't worry. It's not like being in some totally SPICELESS school lesson. LingoPhone is designed to make learning FUN and a REAL HAPPENIN' EXPERIENCE!

What's more, it's HASSLE FREE! You decide what you want to learn, when you want to learn it! And if you can be arsed to learn it! At LingoPhone we're not CONTROL FREAKS!

LingoPhone
Let's Speak Spice

Do I really have to pee into a hotel flower pot?

It was one of the most hilarious moments in the entire Spice saga. Two Spice Girls, who shall remain nameless, were drunk and decided to relieve themselves – into a swanky hotel flower pot! How everyone laughed and the moment passed into Spice legend.

If you seriously want to be a member of the band, then you'll have to get up to japes like this too! Have you got what it takes to urinate in a hotel flower pot? If not, it's unlikely you're Spice Girl material!

So put yourself to the test

STEP 1 GET INTO TRAINING
You can practise safely at home – provided everybody's out and have bad head colds when they do return. If you can't find a suitable flower pot, try the washing up bowl or an empty box of Coco Pops. Avoid using a colander or anything you later have to eat out of. Don't use the television set, especially if it's plugged in.

STEP 3 EARN LOTS OF MONEY
Even one night's stay at the sort of hotel the Fab Five stay at doesn't come cheap. You may need to save for months to be able to urinate there. Try taking on two paper rounds, wash your mum's car every weekend or sell your jewellery.

STEP 3 BOOK INTO A SWANKY HOTEL
You've finally raised the money. Before booking in, check that the hotel does indeed have flower pots that can be urinated into. You'll be surprised how many don't. Also check that they're not filled with tall spikey cacti. Go to your room, consume as much liquid as you can, then sneak out into the corridor in the dead of night. Nerves will probably do the rest for you.

STEP 4 PUSH IT, SISTER!
If you're feeling like prime Spice Girl material, why not go one step further than the Girls – and urinate on something else too while you're there. Most five star hotels offer plenty of things which you can relieve yourself on including the ash trays, shoes left outside the rooms for polishing, morning papers, breakfast trays, toiletry carts and the concierge! You are only limited by your imagination – and your bladder!

STEP 5 WHAT TO SAY WHEN HOTEL SECURITY CATCHES YOU...

...IF YOU'RE A SPICE GIRL

- I'm a member of the Spice Girls – so piss off you little fascist or I'll get you fired
- Got any toilet paper, mate?
- You could sell that pot for a thousand pounds!
- Your mates won't believe you tomorrow!
- Girl Power!

...IF YOU'RE NOT

- Ow! Let go! You're hurting my arm
- I'm not mental! You must believe me!
- Please don't call the police
- Please don't tell my mum!

Is it true that the Spice Girls are into
Devil Worship?

All fantastically famous pop groups and singers are dogged by rumours, some more ridiculous than others:

Group	Rumour
The Doors	Jim Morrison is really alive but in hiding
The Beatles	Paul McCartney is dead
Elastica	Have the A-bomb
Wet Wet Wet	Ate that bloke from the Manic Street Preachers
Kula Shaker	Alien pod-beings here on Earth to observe mankind
D:Ream	Know the secret of the Bermuda Triangle but won't tell
Dodgy	Eat their own weight in seaweed every Thursday
Supergrass	Can turn lead into gold
Prodigy	Sane
Bros	Merchant bankers
Ant and Dec	Are really PJ and Duncan
PJ and Duncan	Are really Alisha's Attic
Jarvis Cocker	Michael Jackson's younger brother
Louise Nurding (ex Eternal)	Michael Howard in drag
Oasis	Continue to provide a refuge for Lord Lucan
East 17	Come from the 25th Century
Jamiroquai	Deliberately named the band just to drive Smash Hits proof-readers mental
Hanson	Can breathe underwater
Milli Vanilli	Don't sing on their own records
Robbie Williams	Really Jim Morrison
Boyzone	Can only survive by drinking the blood of virgins
Blur	Will make good record again one day
Madonna	Has a four foot long willy

In the case of the Spice Girls, there's a long-standing rumour that they're devil worshippers, but the evidence is purely circumstantial. OK, there are those photographs on the Internet of Geri naked in a field but there's absolutely no evidence of a weird black magic ritual going on in the background.

Additionally, the 'B' in Mel B's name does not stand for 'Beelzebub'. Neither does the 'C' in Mel C's name stand for Lucifer – spelt wrong.

The so-called backwards lyrics

You've probably heard those rumours about playing the chorus of 'Wannabe' backwards and hearing 'Satan is my master. Hail to the prince of Darkness'.

This is rubbish and all you get in reality is: 'Sdneirf ym htiw teg attog uoy revol ym eb annaw uoy fi' – which doesn't sound any more evil than the lyric heard the right way round.

The Spice Girls were created to lead men into sin

Hardly likely, as the vast majority of their fans are girls under the age of 5 .

The Spice Girls sold their souls to Satan
NO. TO PEPSI COLA.

'Zigazig-ha'

Not a ritual chant to raise Satan from his slumber but a bit of harmless, innocent nonsense (but don't go saying it at dawn on the summer solstice anyway, OK?)

Victoria
Victoria is not pure evil. She's just a bit grumpy sometimes.

What's it really like in a recording studio?

The first thing that you notice about the recording studio is that it's full of nobs. Most of these work for the record company but the rest are used to make adjustments to the sound. You don't need to worry about the technical side of recording. There are people who get paid a thousand times less than you to worry about that. What's more important, though, is that you know who you have to be nice to (the producer) and who you can afford to upset (everyone else).

The producer has to make sure that the song you're recording is a number 1, or at least, a top 5 hit. He tells the musicians how to play, the singers (i.e. you) how to sing and the engineers how to engineer.

Recording artistes are sensitive souls, so the producer has to be diplomatic when he's criticizing people – people like you. That's why most of the time what he says to you isn't what he really means.

N.B. Saying 'One, Two, One, Two' into the mike is a dead giveaway that you've never been in a studio before. This is not the way that sound levels are tested. It is just a punchline to the joke 'How many musicians does it take to change a lightbulb?'

What the producer says to you
WHAT THE PRODUCER REALLY MEANS

'Not bad, not bad'
'THAT WAS *&$#£% AWFUL'

'Once more from the top'
'AT LEAST ANOTHER 5 MORE TIMES FROM THE TOP. MAYBE THEN YOU'LL GET IT RIGHT'

'Brilliant!'
'IT WILL HAVE TO DO. YOU'VE JUST USED UP ALL THE STUDIO BUDGET AND, ANYWAY, I'VE GOT A HOT DATE TONIGHT'

'Let's try it a slightly different way now'
'LET'S TRY IT THE BEST WAY; THE WAY I WANTED TO DO IT RIGHT FROM THE BEGINNING'

'That sounded really interesting'
'THAT SOUNDED REALLY UNCOMMERCIAL'

'That's a good idea'
'THAT'S A REALLY CRAPPY IDEA BUT I'LL HUMOUR YOU BECAUSE YOU'RE THE RECORD COMPANY'S TOP ACT'

'That's a good question'
'I CAN'T BELIEVE ANYONE CAN BE THAT DUMB!'

'That was fine, but let's try it in C this time'
'MY GOD! SHE WAS ACTUALLY SINGING IT IN M!!!!!!!!!!!!!!!!!!!!!!!!!!!!!'

'Don't worry about that. We'll fix it in the mix'
'DON'T WORRY ABOUT THAT. BY THE TIME WE DUB OVER THE SESSION SINGERS NO ONE WILL BE ABLE TO HEAR YOU ANYWAY'

'Yes. We could arrange it like that'
'OVER MY DEAD BODY'

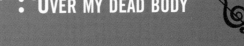

How Can I Be Like –
Ginger Spice?

- Eat loads and loads and loads of carrots (alternatively, buy loads and loads and loads of hair dye, like Clairol 'CopperNob' or SupaShine 'It Didn't Look Like That On The Packet')
- Smear Vaseline or Mazola liberally all over face to achieve that all-important 'shiny' look
- Heaving cleavage (to get the look stuff two agitated ferrets down your trainer bra)

GET THE LOOK! #2

- Have all your back teeth removed to achieve Cheek Bone Nirvana
- Dress like you've got absolutely no sense of style
- Or taste
- Or colour
- Or hand and eye co-ordination
- Wear four-inch soles to break that all important psychological 'five foot' barrier

GERI HAS...

- Redder than red hair
- Passion
- Determination
- More skeletons in the closet than the Royal Medical School
- A wardrobe Charles Manson would be proud of
- Lots of money

MORE TIPZ!

Get some tattoos. Geri has two, and claims that they're very spiritual – but then, she is the nutty one in the group!

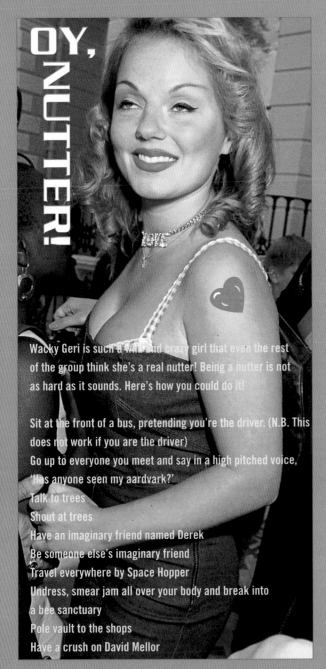

OY, NUTTER!

Wacky Geri is such a wild and crazy girl that even the rest of the group think she's a real nutter! Being a nutter is not as hard as it sounds. Here's how you could do it!

Sit at the front of a bus, pretending you're the driver. (N.B. This does not work if you are the driver)
Go up to everyone you meet and say in a high pitched voice, 'Has anyone seen my aardvark?'
Talk to trees
Shout at trees
Have an imaginary friend named Derek
Be someone else's imaginary friend
Travel everywhere by Space Hopper
Undress, smear jam all over your body and break into a bee sanctuary
Pole vault to the shops
Have a crush on David Mellor

PASSION IS THE FASHION

Geri says, 'We feel passionate about everything!' and, since red heads are noted for being emotional and excitable, it must be true. If you also want to feel passionate about everything, that's a cool vibe – but if you feel that you're not ready for it that's OK too. After all, no matter how much respect you have, it's difficult to get passionate about everything.

These are things it's easy to get passionate about, like Geri:
- Relationships
- Designer clothes
- The urge to succeed at all costs
- Burning ambition
- Money

These are things it's NOT easy to get passionate about, even though Geri manages:
- Custard Creams
- Toilet Duck
- Mighty White bread
- Zebra crossings
- Waste disposal units
- Crazy paving
- Sparrows
- Woolworths
- The Bolivian-Chile trade war

Can I really make a load o %MONEY being a Spice Girl?

If you're a Spice Girl, making music and spreading the Girl Power vibe is what being in the group is all about. Shame on you if your biggest motivation for joining is the thought of earning a totally absolute mega kicking fortune. If you do, that's just a fringe benefit. Don't let it get in the way of being yourself and being true to your roots.

So just how wealthy are the Spice Girls? We asked the top financial wizards and money gurus:

LOCATION OF WORLD'S 11 LARGEST CURRENCY RESERVES

1 Fort Knox Bullion reserves, Kentucky, USA
2 Basle Central Clearing Bank, Switzerland
3 Holocaust Victims Deposit Account, Geneva, Switzerland
4 Bottom of Emma's handbag, England
5 Mel C's biscuit barrel, England
6 Imperial Bank of Saudi
7 Behind the clock in Mel B's living room, England
8 Stuffed down Geri's bra, England
9 A big shoe box under Victoria's bed, England
10 Sultan of Brunei's Number 253 Account
11 Down the back of Emma's sofa, England

'I intend to introduce a new Spice Girls tax – to be levied on the Spice Girls. If I put an extra 1% on their income tax I can pay for the National Health Service. I'm doing this to stop the economy from overheating – and because I hate them.'

Gordon Brown
(Chancellor of the Exchequer and Ungroovy Person)

'The Bank of England is pleased to announce significant cost savings. Rather than using hundreds and hundreds of armoured cars to deliver £20 notes to banks and building societies we just send them all direct to the Spice Girls.'

Eddie George
(Governor, Bank of England)

'I'm one of the world's most influential currency brokers. I have the ability to destroy economies and topple governments. I thought I was powerful until I realized how much the Spice Girls earn. Now I feel like an ant.'

John deSilva
(One of the World's Most Influential Currency Brokers)

I've heard that the Spice Girls are vital to Britain's balance of trade

You've heard right! The Spice Girls are not only Britain's biggest export earner, but they're proud to be British! Without the dosh they bring in to the country we might see income tax rise to 99%, £300 go on a packet of cigarettes and £100 on a bottle of alcopops! That's how thankful you should be for them.

When you look at this chart you can see how important they really are to Britain's economy:

BRITAIN'S EXPORTS	VALUE TO ECONOMY
Spice Girls white plastic bum bags	£517,000,000
Spice Girls key rings	£496,000,000
Spice Girls records	£419,000,000
Spent plutonium fuel rods	£320,000,000
Infected beef carcasses	£274,000,000
Illegal electric shock batons	£271,000,000
Dangerous power stations for Third World countries	£212,000,000
Surface to air missiles for Iran	£182,000,000
Land mines	£163,000,000
Paintings that really should belong to the nation	£110,000,000
Overpriced and shoddy electrical goods	£87,000,000
'Guardsman' and 'Policeman' souvenir teddy bears	£84,000,000
Healthy kidneys and livers for rich Arabs who are dying	£68,000,000
Warm and slightly acidic Real Ale	£61,000,000
All the manky mackerels that the Spanish have left behind	£45,000,000
Premier League footballers	£39,000,000
Cricket balls	£7,000,000
Croquet sets	£2,000,000

The future is female: #5

THE SPICE GIRLS REACH OUT TO THE LITTLE ONES...

The Spice Girls aren't just popular with billions and billions of sophisticated teenagers and hip adults. Their songs and philosophy have also captured the imaginations of the under-fives as never before! Next year, the Spice Girls' younger fans can look forward to a very special series of brilliant books aimed straight at them, featuring the irresistible and v. perky Little Spice.

DO NOT LEARN THESE WORDS. THEY ARE BAD WORDS
BOOTLEG **BORROW** BOYZONE DEFERRED GRATIFICATION
ETERNAL GULLIBLE HOME-TAPING **HYPE** JUNK MARKET-STALL
OVERPRICED SAVE SHODDY UNOFFICIAL

THE 'LITTLE SPICE' FIRST EASY READER

BUY THE BOOK

SHE HAS CASH

WE LOVE LITTLE SPICE

THIS IS LITTLE SPICE

BUY THE VIDEO

GOOD LITTLE SPICE

GIRL POWER!

BUY THE CD

WE LOVE
LITTLE
SPICE

BUY THE PHOTO
ALBUM

OTHER BOOKS IN THIS SERIES
Little Spice Goes Shopping
Little Spice Goes Shopping Again
Little Spice and Her Friends Go Shopping
Little Spice Meets Ginger Spice (And Goes Shopping)
Little Spice Gets Her Pocket Money
Little Spice Writes Her Christmas List
Little Spice Writes Her Birthday List
Little Spice Meets Kindly Uncle Dave
Little Spice Finds A Tenner
Little Spice and The Evil Piggy Bank

There'll even
be bedtime
story books for
youngsters who
just can't get
enough of the
Fab Five.
Here's a sneak
preview! Don't
tell anyone we
showed you....

SPICE GIRLS
BEDTIME STORIES

JANE AND HER WICKED MOTHER

Once upon a time there was a little girl called Jane who had a very wicked mother who wouldn't buy her any Spice Girls Merchandise. What a horrid mum! Horrid and wicked and ugly and diseased!

Jane had set her heart on the absolutely hip and trendy new Spice Girls Tote Bag (£16.99 plus £2.50 towards postage and packing. All major credit cards accepted) which you can see advertised at the back of this book, along with lots of other highly collectable and unmissable must-have Spice-tastic goodies! However, her evil mummy refused to pay for the bag. She mumbled something about the Spice Girls 'being a bad influence' and 'not wanting to hear a six year old singing 'If you wannabe my lover' – but the truth is she just wasn't vibey and living large.

Luckily, Jane knew what to do, because she lived the Spice life and had girl power.

First she scowled like Posh Spice, then she acted like a big baby just like Emma. Then she did high kicks all around the room like Sporty, smashing things, then she went mental and took all her clothes off like Geri and finally she shouted and shouted just like Mel B!

When Jane's mum saw how dedicated to the Spice-O-Sphere little Jane was, she relented and bought the bag (£16.99 plus £2.50 towards postage and packing. All major credit cards accepted) – and from that day on, Jane loved her mummy.

Girl power had done its magic and brought mummy and Jane together again! Massive!

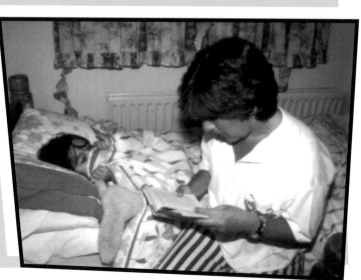

What should I wear?

Being a Spice Girl is all about dressing how you want – so throw away your wardrobe and let's get slick 'n' Spicey!

Get into practice – design your own Spice Girls look at home!

Buy a big heap of stuff from Oxfam. Take it home, blindfold yourself, shuffle it all up, then select your outfit at random. You know you've got it right when:

- IT UPSETS YOUR MUM
- YOUR LITTLE SISTER HAS A FIT OF THE GIGGLES AT THE DINNER TABLE AND DIET COKE STARTS COMING OUT OF HER NOSE
- YOU DON'T DARE LOOK IN THE MIRROR
- FRIENDS START TO DESERT YOU
- YOU DAREN'T GO OUT IN THE STREET
- SOMEONE COMES UP TO YOU AND SAYS 'OH, I DIDN'T KNOW THEY WERE BACK IN FASHION'
- YOU GET MISTAKEN FOR A PROSTITUTE WITH NO DRESS SENSE
- THE DEPARTMENT OF THE ENVIRONMENT DECLARES YOU AN OFFICIAL EYESORE

Spice Chic!

RIGHT
- Something that looks cheap – but most certainly isn't
- Something that looks nasty – and most certainly is

WRONG
- Anything that costs 50p a week for 14 weeks out of the Gratton catalogue
- Anything you're wearing at the moment
- Anything you can afford

Scary Spice?

HUGE GOB (TRY MOUTH-STRETCHING EXERCISES. BEGIN BY FITTING IN A BILLIARD BALL. END UP WITH A MOUTH WIDE ENOUGH TO COMFORTABLY ACCOMMODATE A 22" SONY TRINTRON TV WITH REMOTE CONTROL)

GROW BIG HAIR, BIGGER THAN MICHAEL JACKSON IN THE EARLY DAYS AND EVEN BIGGER THAN THE LEADER IN THE HAIR BEAR BUNCH. ALTERNATIVELY, LET SOME CARE IN THE COMMUNITY PATIENT GO AT YOU WITH A PAIR OF CRIMPING TONGS

HAVE YOUR TONGUE PIERCED (USEFUL FOR WAGGLING AND MAKING PEOPLE FEEL GROSS)

GET A CHINESE TATTOO ON STOMACH THAT MEANS 'INNER HARMONY' (UNTIL YOU HAVE A BABY, THEN THE STRETCH MARKS WILL TURN IT INTO 'AJHD KAJDKJSLFKLO SASKDSDFLDLFKLDS')

TALK the TALK!
It doesn't matter what you say, as long as you sound like Nora Batty and shout everything at 125 decibels.

GET THE LOOK! #3

BUY LOADS OF ETHNIC JEWELLERY TO 'ACKNOWLEDGE YOUR ROOTS' (AND BECAUSE IT'S DEAD CHEAP)

WEAR GLASSES IN AN EFFORT TO MAKE YOU LOOK INTELLIGENT. N.B. THIS DOESN'T ALWAYS WORK

GET SOME BOOTS SO BIG THAT THEY'D MAKE IT LOOK LIKE JUDGE DREDD GOT HIS FROM START RITE

FIERCE AND PIERCED!

MEL B HAS...

- Ferocity
- Animal magnetism
- Guts
- 54 leopard-skin bikinis
- A voice that could fell trees
- Lungs with the capacity of a Graf Zeppelin
- A hole in her tongue the size of a fifty pence piece
- A misconception that she's leader of the group
- Lots of money

Mel B had her tongue pierced so, if you want to be like her, so should you. Tongue piercing doesn't have to be expensive – so long as you don't mind getting septicaemia, talking with a lisp and dribbling for the rest of your life. In theory you could do it at home using an office hole punch – but then again, in theory, you could walk to the Sun.

None of the other Spice Girls – not even Geri – has their tongue pierced, so you can tell how sensible this is.

MORE TIPZ!

By her own admission, Mel B is foul-mouthed. Now you've probably heard that swearing isn't big and it isn't clever (rather like Baby Spice) but with Girl Power, it's just another way of saying what you feel like, when you feel like it. It's easy to be foul-mouthed like Scary Spice:

At school:
Teacher: Can anyone tell me what the capital of the Netherlands is?
You: Bum hole!

ARSE!

On the bus:
Conductor: Can I see your tickets please?
You: Toss!

At home:
Mum: Dinner's served!
You: Twot!

At your Saturday job:
Customer: Do you have this in a size 10?
You: Titties!

I'm still not sure that I understand Girl Power. Can you explain it to me in simple terms (*please*)?

Look, don't worry if you don't understand what it's all about right away. No one said you had to be a brain box to join the Spice Girls, did they? See if this beginner's guide tells it like it is for you.

This is Janet

This is John

John is wearing the clothes his mummy bought him.
He likes these clothes.
Janet thinks John's clothes suck.
Suck. Suck. Suck.
She chooses her own clothes.
Her clothes are Kicking.

Janet and John like music.
John likes 'The Ugly Ducking', 'The Laughing Policeman' and 'Sparky's Magic Piano'.
Janet likes anything by the Spice Girls.
Janet's mummy tells her not to play her music loud.
Janet plays her music loud. Loud. Loud. Loud.
Janet doesn't care what her mummy says.
Janet follows her own groove.

When John grows up, he wants to be a policeman.
'Stop Thief!' 'Evening all.' His teachers think he will be a good policeman.
When Janet grows up she wants to be a pop singer.
Her teacher tells her not to be so silly.
But Girl Power can make dreams come true.
True. True. True.
(If you're very lucky.)
No jobs stacking shelves at Safeway for Janet!

John's a swot.
Read, John, Read.
He's a boy. He must work.
Janet is Large. She bunks off.
She has Girl Power.
She will earn millions when she is a star.
Who needs GCSEs?
It's the Girl Power promise.
Promise. Promise. Promise.
And we know the Spice Girls never lie.

There. That should have made Girl Power easy to understand. Easy. Easy. Easy. Just for you.

57

What's it really like being in the Spice Girls?

Play this groovy game – and enjoy all the thrills, chills and spills as you share the girls' rise to superstardom. It's almost like being there alongside Mel B and the gang – if you've got a really strong imagination!

HOW TO PLAY

Get together with some cool friends. Less cool friends can watch.

You'll each need a token. Symbolically, it's best to use pound coins to represent the Spice Girls but – if you're poor – buttons will do. You'll also need a dice.

Put your tokens on the 'Complete Non-Entity' square. To start, you each shake a dice. The highest score goes first, then the second highest and so on. Every time you land on a GIRL POWER! space, your natural talent propels your career on to new and dizzying heights – but watch out for the uncool CAREER CRISIS! spaces – or you could find your latest album in the bargain bins!

The first person to reach 'International Superstardom' wins! May the Spice be with you!

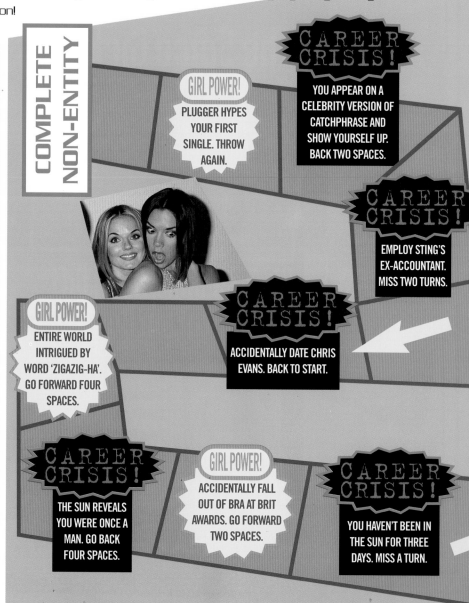

COMPLETE NON-ENTITY

GIRL POWER!
PLUGGER HYPES YOUR FIRST SINGLE. THROW AGAIN.

CAREER CRISIS!
YOU APPEAR ON A CELEBRITY VERSION OF CATCHPHRASE AND SHOW YOURSELF UP. BACK TWO SPACES.

CAREER CRISIS!
EMPLOY STING'S EX-ACCOUNTANT. MISS TWO TURNS.

GIRL POWER!
ENTIRE WORLD INTRIGUED BY WORD 'ZIGAZIG-HA'. GO FORWARD FOUR SPACES.

CAREER CRISIS!
ACCIDENTALLY DATE CHRIS EVANS. BACK TO START.

CAREER CRISIS!
THE SUN REVEALS YOU WERE ONCE A MAN. GO BACK FOUR SPACES.

GIRL POWER!
ACCIDENTALLY FALL OUT OF BRA AT BRIT AWARDS. GO FORWARD TWO SPACES.

CAREER CRISIS!
YOU HAVEN'T BEEN IN THE SUN FOR THREE DAYS. MISS A TURN.

Is it true the Spice Girls are more totally fab than the Beatles?

You betcha! If anyone pokes fun at you for wanting to join the Spice Girls, like saying that they're not a 'serious' group, just point out that they're actually a million, billion miles better than that has-been boy band the Beatles! And that's no exaggeration.

Think about it. The Fab Five has just gotta be better than a measly Fab Four! And it doesn't end there!

- 'ZIGAZIG-HA' (FROM 'WANNABE') IS A MUCH MORE MEANINGFUL LYRIC THAN 'GOOGOOGAJOOB' ('I AM THE WALRUS')!

- THE BEATLES, THROUGHOUT THEIR LONG HISTORY, NEVER ONCE WON A BRIT AWARD – OR TOPPED A SMASH HITS READERS' POLL!

- THE SPICE GIRLS ARE BANG UP TO DATE BUT THE BEATLES BROKE UP NEARLY THIRTY YEARS AGO!

- THE SPICES HAVE ALREADY MADE MORE MONEY THAN THE BEATLES, SO THEY MUST BE BETTER!

- THE BEATLES NEVER HAD GIRL POWER!

- THE BEATLES ONLY HAD TWO SONGWRITERS WHEREAS THE SPICE GIRLS HAVE ELEVEN!

- YOU CAN'T 'SLAM YOUR BODY DOWN AND WIND IT ALL AROUND' TO 'YESTERDAY'

- DURING THEIR CAREER, THE BEATLES NEVER SOLD A MILLION VIDEOS (THEY NEVER EVER SOLD ONE)

- NOT ONE MEMBER OF THE BEATLES WORE A TIGHT FITTING UNION JACK DRESS AND HUGE RED BOOTS

- NO BEATLES FAN EVER HAD THE OPPORTUNITY TO BUY AN INDISPENSABLE 'OFFICIAL' WHITE PLASTIC MINI RUCK SACK FOR £19.99

- THE SPICE GIRLS ARE MUCH MORE POLITICALLY CORRECT, HAVING TWO MEMBERS FROM ETHNIC MINORITIES; MEL B (WHO'S OF MIXED RACE) AND GERI (WHO'S GINGER)!

- UNLIKE THE BEATLES, THE SPICE GIRLS HAVE NEVER CLAIMED TO BE 'MORE POPULAR THAN JESUS'. EVERYONE KNOWS THEY ARE!

- IT TOOK THREE SINGLES BEFORE THE BEATLES GOT TO NUMBER 1. THE FIRST THREE SPICE GIRLS SINGLES REACHED THE TOP SLOT!

- ALL THE SPICE GIRLS HAVE NICKNAMES WHEREAS JUST ONE OF THE BEATLES DID (AND 'RINGO' IS A PRETTY NAFF NICKNAME ANYWAY)

- THE BEATLES WERE NEVER ONCE INVITED TO SWITCH ON THE OXFORD STREET CHRISTMAS LIGHTS!

- OR LAUNCH CHANNEL 5!

- FOUR OF THE SPICE GIRLS ARE TALLER THAN RINGO

- THE SPICE GIRLS HAVEN'T SPLIT UP (YET)!

THE FUTURE IS FEMALE: #6
HOW WILL GIRL POWER CHANGE THE WORLD?

There's never been anything quite like the Girl Power phenomenon.
It's changing the world as we speak!
Brainy sociologists are already rushing to understand the new trend.

WHAT THE EXPERTS SAY:

'We used to think a person's life would be determined by the interaction of a complex number of factors,' says one, 'including upbringing, education opportunities, physical appearance, gender roles, ethnicity, social skills, health, personality, labelling, childhood experiences, parental expectations, localized job opportunities, genetics and social economic grouping.

'Boy, did the Spices ever put us right about that! It turns out that, as long as you have Girl Power, you can be anything you want to be!

'That's why we're now predicting that, by the year 2005, over 17 million young girls will be singing in girl groups in the UK!'

DID YOU KNOW?: #2

If you took all the money the Spice Girls have made and piled it up in a big heap – they'd get the police to arrest you.

Of course, this will change the world beyond all recognition.

IN THE NEW 'GIRL POWER' WORLD:

- EACH EPISODE OF TOP OF THE POPS WILL BE **15** DAYS LONG!
- NEWSAGENTS WILL HAVE TO BE **6** MILES WIDE TO STOCK ALL THE POSTER MAGAZINES
- THE VIRGIN MEGASTORE WILL BE THE SIZE OF WALES
- QUEUES OUTSIDE THE WEMBLEY ARENA WILL STRETCH BACK **15** MILES — AS GIRL GROUPS LINE UP TO PLAY
- EACH COPY OF SMASH HITS MAGAZINE WILL WEIGH THE SAME AS A ROYAL NAVY DESTROYER
- THE PREMIER LEAGUE WILL HAVE TO EXPAND ITS SIZE TO **60,000** CLUBS IN ORDER TO SATISFY THE DEMAND FOR BOYFRIENDS

OF COURSE THERE WILL BE DRAWBACKS:

- EVERY GIRL WILL BE SO RICH THAT THE WHOLE OF THE AMAZON RAIN FOREST WILL HAVE TO BE TORN DOWN TO MAKE ALL THE £50 NOTES NEEDED
- YOU WILL HAVE TO WAIT AN AWFULLY LONG TIME TO GET SERVED IN WOOLWORTHS OR TO HAVE YOUR HAIR DONE
- THERE'LL BE A **600**-YEAR WAITING LIST FOR PORSCHES
- PIG IRON WILL BECOME MORE EXPENSIVE, POUND FOR POUND, THAN GOLD — AS DEMAND FOR NOSE AND TONGUE STUDS OUTSTRIPS SUPPLY
- THERE WILL BE ANOTHER OIL CRISIS AS OPEC DIVERTS **50,000,000,000** BARRELS A YEAR OVER TO MANUFACTURING PLASTIC CD CASES
- BY **2004** EVERY SINGLE POSSIBLE NAME FOR A GIRL BAND WOULD HAVE BEEN SNAPPED UP AND UNLUCKY GROUPS WILL HAVE TO BE KNOWN BY **25** DIGIT ALPHANUMERIC CODES — OR A SERIES OF COMPLICATED CLICKING NOISES MADE WITH THE TONGUE

Spice Merchandise!

I MIGHT BE KNOWN AS POSH SPICE, BUT THAT DOESN'T STOP ME LIKING A BIT OF ROUGH SOMETIMES!

THAT'S WHY THE NEW SPICE GIRLS SANDPAPER IS ALWAYS MY SANDPAPER OF CHOICE!

AVAILABLE FROM ALL GOOD **DIY** STORES AND RECORD SHOPS.

DID YOU KNOW?: #3

Victoria once had her knickers ripped off and thrown out the window of a speeding taxi – and she's the posh one!

HOW SHOULD I DEAL WITH THE PRESS WHEN I'M FAMOUS?

In a word, cooperate.

The tabloid press can make or break your career so it's best to work with them, not against them. Sometimes the press can be your best friend. Sometimes it can be your worst enemy. Other times it can be like an ex-boyfriend, a neighbour, that nice lady at the Building Society, your younger brother or just someone you met on holiday.

Whatever the press is, the Spice Girls are currently the tabloids' darlings and the papers hang on their every word...

What the tabloids LOVE Spice Girls to have:

- Loads of bitter ex-boyfriends (who kept diaries and a pile of Polaroids)
- A very, very, very bitter ex-manager in desperate need of cash
- A ballooning weight problem
- Surreptitious plastic surgery
- A photogenic mum
- A father who walked out on them when they were four
- A vendetta against another girl group
- A view on politics, however naive and simplistic
- A history of nude modelling
- A fling with a sportsman
- A fling with a soap star
- A penchant for dressing up in their favourite football team's strip
- Loads and loads of photos of them when they were young
- Shocking amounts of cash
- The promise of earning more
- Strong opinions on the Lottery

What you said

I took two aspirin for my headache··········
I think William Hague's really cute*··········
I lost weight during the last tour··········
My ex-boyfriend still writes to me··········
I got locked in my hotel room by mistake·····
I haven't seen my boyfriend for a week·······
Paul Ince and Teddy Sheringham are good·····
mates of mine
I love my mum!··········
I love watching Eastenders··········

What the tabloids HATE Spice Girls to have:

A press agent who gives exclusivity to a rival paper

What the tabloids are not remotely interested in:

- Their music
- What they think of Page 3
- What they actually said...

What the paper printed

- Spice Girl's drugs shame
- Spice Girls back Tories!
- Spice Girl in anorexia shock!
- Spice Girl in stalker horror!
- Spice Girl in bondage shame!
- Spice Girl dumps lover!
- Spice Girl in three-in-a-bed romp with England players!
- I hate my mum!
- Spice Girl's fling with Eastenders Bad Boy!

Er... Wot?

* THIS IS JUST AN EXAMPLE. WE KNOW THAT NO ONE'S MAD ENOUGH TO ACTUALLY SAY THIS (NOT EVEN GERI)

How can I be 'in yer face' at press conferences?

Today, it's not enough to make great sounds to have a hit. You must also master the art of selling yourself. This is something that a true Spice Girl knows all about.

You've got to be 'in the public's face' all the time – and that's not easy because there's over 55 million of them in the UK alone and they move around a bit. The best way to get 'in yer face' when it comes to potential record buyers is to hold a press conference and get your message across to the nation.

STUCK FOR WORDS?

•STICK YOUR TONGUE DOWN GERI'S THROAT FOR THE CAMERAS. (IT'LL MAKE A GREAT PHOTO OPPORTUNITY AND – WHO KNOWS? – MAYBE YOU'LL LEARN SOMETHING NEW ABOUT YOURSELF!)

•WAVE YOUR ARMS AND GRIN (ALWAYS A GOOD FALL BACK IF YOU HAVE NOTHING TO SAY)

•SAY 'GIRL POWER!'

•SHOW SOME CLEAVAGE (ALWAYS POPULAR WITH LAZY AND UNTALENTED CAPTION WRITERS WHO CAN FALL BACK ON PUNS ABOUT 'BIG HITS' OR 'OPPORTUNITY KNOCKERS')

DID YOU KNOW?: #

If all the Spice Girls were laid end on end – David Beckham, for one, would be very annoyed!

SELLING YOUR NEW ALBUM

A new album is always

- MEGA
- VIBEY
- MEGA-VIBEY
- VERY SPECIAL TO US
- OUR BEST YET
- WORTH THE WAIT
- OUR FAVOURITE TO DATE
- A DEFINITE STEP FORWARD FOR US
- FOR THE FANS

A new album is never

- SUCKSVILLE
- CONTRACTUALLY OBLIGATED
- A FILLER UNTIL THE 'GREATEST HITS' COMES OUT
- A CASH COW
- THE BEST WE COULD DO GIVEN OUR TOURING COMMITMENTS
- AN ANSWER TO OUR TAX PROBLEMS
- THE CRAP WE LEFT OFF THE LAST ALBUM
- JUST LIKE THE LAST ONE, ONLY NOT AS CATCHY
- SOME OLD TUT WE KNOCKED UP OVER THE WEEKEND
- EXPERIMENTAL
- COVERS OF SOMEONE ELSE'S B-SIDES

Who would be my best mate in the Spice Girls? ....

MEL B

Being mates with Mel B would be great fun! You could go out doing any one of a hundred wild things which you'll later regret! She'd take you to get a really cool tattoo – and you'd get grounded for a year! – or to get your tongue pierced (and you'd end up screaming for a year).

Of course, you could go shopping together, but it wouldn't be much fun because she's got lots of money and you haven't and you'd have to watch her try on these fab clothes that you can't afford . Then you'd lose your temper, say something spiteful and end up going home alone on the bus.

BEST PLACES TO GO FOR FUN: Raunchy night clubs, tongue-piercing and tattoo parlours
MISS OUT ON: The Whispering Gallery at St Pauls
YOU NEED: Stamina, copious amounts of alcohol, earplugs
SHE NEEDS: A horse tranquilliser

MEL C

Hanging out with Mel C would be no absolutely no fun. You'd want to go shopping and she'd want to go on a five mile run. You'd want to stay in but she'd want to work out. You'd want to watch The Chart Show and she'd want to watch Football Italia, (or athletics from Crystal Palace, or table tennis, or rugby or something equally mind-numbingly sporty and therefore non-consequential…).
You could, however, go to concerts together, but then she'd be invited backstage after the gig and you wouldn't and you'd end up waiting outside in the cold and miss the last train home and get a roasting from your mum.

BEST PLACES TO GO FOR FUN: Nowhere
MISS OUT ON: Everything
YOU NEED: To find a new friend
SHE NEEDS: A sports related injury to teach her a few lessons

EMMA

Being best mates with Emma would be like hanging out with your little sister – and you know how much fun that is. Emma would be a good giggle at first – but would probably start getting on your tits within a few minutes.
You could go out on the pull together, but everyone would be interested in her because she's famous and the boys would keep asking if you were anybody and you'd have to say no and then they'd turn their backs on you and she'd end up getting off with the boy you really liked and you'd have too much to drink and be sick in the taxi on the way home.

BEST PLACES TO GO FOR FUN: Fun fairs, Dunkin' Doughnuts
MISS OUT ON: Museums, art galleries, literary launches
YOU NEED: Patience, tolerance
SHE NEEDS: A slap

Geri is the self-confessed nutter of the group. A fiery Leo — and a redhead to boot — you'd be hard pressed to keep up with her antics! Together you could do lots of crazy things which — being a celebrity — she'll get clean away with while you get a series of police cautions.

Geri loves to talk. You can tell Geri your innermost secrets, secure in the knowledge that she's not listening. Try talking about boys. You could tell her about this hunk in Boyzone that you really fancy, and then she'll say that she's met him and tell you the truth about him and you'll refuse to believe her and put your hands over your ears and cry and stamp your feet.

BEST PLACES TO GO FOR FUN: The ice rink, 70s retro discos

MISS OUT ON: Double dating (because your boyfriend will fancy her instead of you and he'll be nasty to you all night and you'll end up shouting at him in the middle of the road)

YOU NEED: A wild sense of humour, a 70s wardrobe

SHE NEEDS: A straight jacket

Victoria wouldn't give you the time of day

An Ex-Spice Girl Speaks!

I might be gay. Can I still be a Spice Girl?

'I WAS THE FIRST GAY SPICE GIRL IN THE BAND BUT WAS CHUCKED OUT AFTER A FEW DAYS. I STILL CAN'T FIGURE OUT WHY.'

DIESEL SPICE

The Complete Spice Girls Song Lyric Generator

If you join the Spice Girls you'll be introduced to this fantastic device, designed to give you a head start in your song-writing career. All you have to do to write any song is select, say, 12 verses and put them in random order. Then after every fourth verse, insert one of the choruses.

And before you can say 'Wannabe', you'll have a hit record on your hands!

VERSES

Mama — you're a special kind of gal
You're my friend and you're my pal

I'm an independent girl, in charge of my
own destiny
And if I don't wanna make a verse rhyme
I don't have to

You might be a multi-millionaire
But I just like you for your hair

Hold you head up. Look real proud
Speak your mind and shout it loud

Say what you want. Say what you feel
Even if it's just asking for a
MacDonald's hamburger meal

Respect is due. You've earned it now
Don't let anyone call you a stupid cow

When your eyes met mine, I could tell
Something between us began to swell

Take control, girl, of your life
Don't wanna end up just a housewife

Tonight is the night that I love you
You're my sweet baby, goo-goo-goo

Attitude is what you've got
And a rather nice, pert little bot

(Insert after
every 4 verses)

CHORUSES

Mummy, mummy, mummy
You're yummy, yummy, yummy
When I was young I was really bad
But I still love you. And my dad

You're totally vibing, 100% wicked
You're Spiced Up and that's true
You say 'What does all that mean?'
I haven't got a clue

Spice it up. To the max
Spice it up. To the max
Spice it up. To the max
Spice it up. To the max. Yeah!

Come on, girl, take a chance
Don't give him a second glance
Get on the floor and dance, dance, dance
La, la, la — la, la, la

We're in a totally happening, kicking groove
Across that dance floor we will move.
We're jumping here. We're leaping there.
We don't even wear no underwear!

Girl Power. It's here to stay
Girl power. It won't go away
Girl Power. What does it mean?
Girl Power. I like green

DID YOU KNOW?: #6

In the official GIRL POWER! book, Mel B says that 'sex is the world'.

We checked on this and it appears she's made a bit of a slip-up! According to leading experts, sex is the act of reproduction between two individuals, while the world is a spacial body comprising some 5,880,000,000,000,000,000,000 gravemetric tonnes with a circumference of 40,070 km and a rotational period of 23 hours, 56 mins, 4.1 seconds.

Still, it's an easy mistake to make!

Can I have a go at writing lyrics?

Not many bands are as multi-talented as the Spice Girls. They sing, they dance, they have their photographs taken a lot. But, what's more, they write their own songs! Yes, after reading some of their lyrics – 'Yeah, I want you' (from 'Say You'll Be There'), 'Slam your body down zigazig-ha' (from 'Wannabe') and 'Wanna make love to you, baby' (from '2 Become 1') – you'll wonder how any band can have so much talent.

A lot of rival girl singers including En Vogue, Eternal – even Joni Mitchell – say it's just not fair. How can they expect to compete? Well, ladies, you'll have to learn to live with it. When it comes to song-writing, the Spice Girls are the next Lennon and McCartney (well, except that they weren't in the Beatles and they're not men).

Is there a secret to song writing success? You betcha! Firstly it's knowing what subjects are good for songs – and which aren't...

Good and Bad Subjects for Spice Girls Songs

GOOD SUBJECTS...

- Your mum
- Anyone else's mum
- Your friends
- Your mum's friends
- Growing up
- Your mum growing up
- Your first love
- Your mum's first love
- Unity and solidarity between female friends
- Unity and solidarity between mums
- Setting your spirit free
- Taking control of your life
- Sticking up for yourself
- Baring your soul

BAD SUBJECTS...

- ☆ Concrete*
- ☆ Flatulence**
- ☆ Vivisection
- ☆ Lack of hygiene
- ☆ Verrucas
- ☆ Cat vomit
- ☆ That big spot on your bottom
- ☆ How you were abused as a child
- ☆ Kiwi fruit
- ☆ Ripping off your fans
- ☆ Anything to do with public toilets
- ☆ Lumbago
- ☆ Car maintenance
- ☆ Double glazing

* This would only be a good subject for a song if you were being paid thousands and thousands of pounds by the Concrete Marketing Board to promote its products.
** Ditto, the Flatulence Marketing Board – if there was one

Spice Merchandise!

YOU NEED YOUR FEET TO DANCE TO THE SPICE GIRLS FAB RECORDS SO IT PAYS TO LOOK AFTER THEM!

NOW YOU CAN PROTECT THEM THE SPICE GIRLS WAY — WITH THE SPICE GIRLS BUNIO-MATIC ELECTRIC FOOT SCRAPER. DEVELOPED ESPECIALLY FOR YOU BY THE SPICE GIRLS (AND TOP CHIROPRACTORS).

AS USED BY EMMA AND MEL C (THOUGH THE ONE YOU GET WILL BE FRESH OUT OF THE FACTORY AND NOT THE ONES THAT THEY'VE ACTUALLY USED, THE ONES THAT ARE GUMMED UP WITH DEAD SKIN, NAIL PARTICLES AND GREEN STUFF).

BEFORE

AFTER

Now you can put your best foot forward at discos, safe in the knowledge that it's clean and freshly scraped!

Removes unsightly and uncomfortable corns, bunions • even veruccas and weeping toe warts • at the touch of a button!

DID YOU KNOW?: #7

If you took all the money the Spice Girls have earned and laid it out around the world • most of it would get stolen the moment you turned your back!

SPICE FAKZ!

Each Spice Girl signs her name a million times a year! (But 75% of those signatures are on credit card slips and another 15% on lucrative contracts from sponsors.)

How Can I Be Like Sporty Spice?

- Wear your hair up in a ponytail (ideal if you've got drab or lifeless hair)
- Get your nose pierced so it looks like you have a huge shiny bogie stuck to the side of it!
- Tattoos are a great way to permanently disfigure yourself at low cost! Mel C has mystic Chinese symbols on her arm which say 'Egg Fried Rice and Crispy Duck for two to take away'.
- Sellotape your breasts down, hard against your rib cage, to achieve that athletic 'ironing board' physique
- Baggy track suit bottoms (ideal for hiding enormous bums! If you don't have an enormous bum, you can still get 'the look' by sticking a cushion or a partially inflated paddling pool down the back of your track suit bottoms)
- Cool trainers you can't afford (unless you shoplift or go to India and buy a similar pair off the toddlers who make them for tuppence a day)

GET THE LOOK! #4

- Oh dear! Intelligent expression! Don't even attempt it

THE BURDEN OF INTELLIGENCE

Oh dear! Sometimes Sporty Spice can look intelligent. No wonder she's the least popular with the boys and people ask what's she doing in the Spice Girls!

Fortunately the other girls have rallied round to help and given her invaluable advice on how to look gormless too! If you look too smart to be in the Spice Girls, try:

- Opening both eyes as wide as they can go, like you're being examined by a clumsy gynaecologist who keeps all his instruments in the fridge!
- Walking around with your ear superglued to your shoulder
- Opening your mouth wide, as if George Clooney had just decided to show you his goodies
- Waving both hands furiously in the air, like you're 16 and drunk on the dance floor in Ibiza
- Sticking your tongue out – like you're four years old

HOW TO BE 'SPORTY'

Sometimes it seems like boys have monopolised all the good things in life, like motor bikes, sports and self-abuse – but it doesn't have to be that way! Girls can like sports too – as Sporty Spice proves!

To start off with, try watching footie on the telly as it's supposed to be v. trendy at the moment. Follow these simple tips:

- Don't expect very much
- Use two matchsticks to prop your eyelids open
- Switch your brain off
- Don't attempt a Second Division match at first. A coma is serious
- Never smoke while watching Match of the Day, in case you fall asleep
- If watching with your boyfriend, avoid asking stupid questions like, 'How many points do you get for a goal?' or 'Why are those players tonguing each other?'

- Don't try to work out who's who. It doesn't matter
- Don't try to understand 'offside'. No one does
- Don't make remarks about players' thighs. Men don't like to see their idols in that way
- Try to develop an interest in spitting. It helps
- If you find your concentration going, try jabbing knitting needles into your ears or setting fire to your slippers
- Pretend you enjoyed it

TIPZ!

When posing for group photographs, stand to one side and look like you don't quite belong.

MEL C HAS...

- STRENGTH
- INTELLIGENCE
- A SMALL HOLE IN THE SIDE OF HER NOSE
- EXCEPTIONAL LUCK TO HAVE BEEN CHOSEN FOR THE SPICE GIRLS IN THE FIRST PLACE
- PLENTY OF SIGNED PHOTOGRAPHS LEFT
- LOTS OF MONEY

My friends don't like the Spice Girls.
What should I do?

Friends are the most important people in your life – after your mum. The Spice Girls are all best friends and believe that loyalty to your mates is the most important thing there is. You must never, ever let them down!

However, in this case it sounds like you've got the wrong friends! Time to say so long – and get some better ones! It might be tough, but they're holding you back, girl.

✳ ✳ ✳ ✳ ✳

WHAT'S WRONG WITH MY BEST FRIEND?

Stick her picture here...

ARE YOU STUCK WITH A SECOND RATE BESTFRIEND?

Here are some reasons why you might hate her. Tick them off if you agree! Three or more ticks and it's time to say ciao!

[ ] NO ONE ELSE LIKES HER
[ ] SHE SMELLS
[ ] SHE'S NOT PRETTY ENOUGH
[ ] BOYS DON'T LIKE HER

[ ] She wears cheap clothes
[ ] She's totally not cool
[ ] She's fat
[ ] She talks with her mouth full
[ ] People laugh at her
[ ] She's Queen Bitch of the entire universe
[ ] She has stupid hair
[ ] She can't do make up properly
[ ] She doesn't like Neighbours
[ ] She's a swot
[ ] She's never got any money
[ ] She can't dance
[ ] She won't lend me her tapes
[ ] She's called something stupid like Lavinia

WHAT GOOD FRIENDS SAY

✔ There's someone here I'd like you to meet – Brad Pitt
✔ Vodka frenzy!
✔ Do you want my spare front row ticket and back stage pass to the Spice Girls gig?
✔ I couldn't think what to buy you, so here's a cheque for £250
✔ Let's go out on a rave!
✔ Let's get blasted tonight
✔ You really look good!
✔ My dad's lending me the convertible
✔ My sister's Mel B's best friend
✔ My sister's Mel B

WHAT GOOD FRIENDS DON'T SAY

✘ I can't go out tonight, I'm studying
✘ I know it's 3 a.m. but I've just swallowed 300 aspirins...
✘ Your boyfriend really knows how to snog!
✘ I couldn't think what to buy you, so here's a bound volume of Shakespeare
✘ I have to be home by 8.30
✘ Wow! I've slimmed down to a size 18!
✘ Just a lemonade for me, I think
✘ I love you and I don't care what people think!
✘ Hey! Aren't these bright orange pop socks great?
✘ Pop music is the devil's work!
✘ Have you put on weight or is it water retention?

IF YOU NEED SOME HELP IN FINDING NEW FRIENDS, HERE ARE SOME TOP TIPS:

WHERE TO FIND GOOD FRIENDS

✔ In expensive clothes shops
✔ At trendy parties and night clubs
✔ In the most exclusive hairdressers in town
✔ In the front row at top gigs
✔ At a top model agency

HOW YOU CAN BE FRIENDS WITH THE SPICE GIRLS!

✳ Buy all their records (on CD and cassette)
✳ Join their official fan club
✳ Buy all the official Spice Girls merchandise you can afford...
✳ ...then borrow money off your mum to buy more...
✳ ...then off your dad to get the rest
✳ Stay loyal to them when the inevitable media backlash starts
✳ Drink Pepsi Cola

WHERE NOT TO FIND GOOD FRIENDS

The school chess club
Checking out the 'Under £1' rack at Oxfam
The library
Serving behind the counter at the local burger bar
In bed with your dad

Wow! You've just joined the coolest gang in the world!

How Can I Be Like BABY SPICE

• LEAVE YOUR ROOTS SHOWING

• KEEP YOUR GOO-GOO EYES BIG AND VACANT (TRY RECITING BOYZONE LYRICS IN YOUR MIND IF IT HELPS)

• WEAR YOUR HAIR IN LITTLE GIRL BUNCHES, EVEN THOUGH YOU LOOK 38

• GET SOMEONE TO REPEATEDLY PUNCH YOU IN THE FACE SO YOU CAN HAVE A CUTE SNUB NOSE LIKE THIS

• SLOUCH THOSE SHOULDERS! BOYS DON'T LIKE TALL GALS!

• WEAR BRIGHT BLUE NAIL POLISH (EMMA'S FAVE IS BOOTS'S 'SHUT YOUR FINGERS IN A DOOR')

• GRIN LIKE YOU'RE MENTAL. IT MAY STRAIN THE FACIAL MUSCLES, BUT BOYS JUST LOVE IT!

GET THE LOOK!

• WEAR SOMETHING GHASTLY THAT LOOKS LIKE IT CAME FROM TOTS AT C&A

• WEAR A SKIRT SO SHORT THAT IT MAKES EVEN THE HORNIEST OF MEN FEEL ILL

EMMA HAS...

• Charm
• Innocence
• The fashion sense of a tree stump
• The intelligence to match
• A confusing message for young girls
• A very obvious message for sick men
• Lots of money

BE NICE TO MUM!

'I get on really, really well with my mum so she doesn't nag me or tell me to do anything' - Emma

Emma is especially close to her mum and loves being nice to her! Here's some fab ideas for how you can be nice to your mum...

- Speak to her
- Pay for her face lift so she looks better
- Hide your drugs
- Use reliable contraception
- Avoid tell-tale stains on your knicks!
- Tell her that stupid haircut really suits her
- Stop seducing her boyfriends
- Don't come home at 3.30 in the morning and vomit on her best linen
- Don't use her towel when you've got thrush
- Smoke out of the bedroom window so she can't smell it
- Go to school once in a while
- Wait a few more years before getting that groovy facial tattoo
- Spend at least one hour every Sunday off the sofa
- Pretend to be interested when she tells you about when she was your age
- Be tolerant when she calls scrummy Peter Andre a 'thick, greasy little prat'

TALK the TALK!

Try saying...
Tee•hee!
Giggle•giggle!
Chortle•chortle!
Kissie•kissie!
I don't know • I'm only a girl

DID YOU KNOW?: #8

Victoria auditioned for the part of 'Tank Girl' ...and Emma auditioned for the part of the tank!

I know the spice girls really, really love their mums? Is my mum good enough?

It takes someone really special to be a Spice Girls mum. She has to be very supportive through the good times and the bad.

Frankly, most mums don't measure up. Be honest. Your mum probably tries her best, but does she sound as good as Emma's mum? Or Mel B's? How can you go before the press and rave about your mum if she's a bit ordinary?

If you wanna get on in the Spice Girls, you need a first rate mum – the best mum money can buy!

If you're looking for a quick and simple solution, try the Yellow Pages. There are now dozens of enterprising companies offering mums for hire.

IF YOU CAN AFFORD IT, WHY NOT GO THE WHOLE HOG AND **BUY** A COMPLETELY NEW MUM...

YOU'VE TRIED THE REST — NOW TRY THE BEST! EVERY MUM A BARGAIN!

SAVE ££££ ££££'s

RICKY'S MUMS – THE USED MUM SPECIALISTS

THE FORECOURT, 40, THE HIGH ROAD, CHESHUNT

TRADE IN YOUR OLD MUM! GENEROUS PART EXCHANGE DEALS ALWAYS AVAILABLE ON MUMS IN FULL WORKING ORDER OR OLD BANGERS AS SCRAP!

- Full service histories
- Six month guarantee parts and labour
- Cleaned and polished before sale

WE'RE THE BIGGEST BECAUSE WE'RE THE BEST!!!

MUM OF THE MONTH!

SHIRLEY. Unrepeatable bargain! One previous owner. Doesn't shout. Good starter in morning. Excellent condition. SOTE, TOB, OT, FSIP, DYAA, FCOB. £1,200 ONO

DORIS. NICE FAMILY MUM. GENUINE REASON FOR SALE. OP. LHA. IB. WG. DW. £950 ONO

GWEN. HURRY – FIRST TO SEE WILL BUY! G. COND. NS. CCF. SD. SETTF. STYHLG. £599 ONO

CAROL. GOOD RUNNER (TO SHOPS FOR FISH AND CHIPS, CIGARETTES, ETC.) SETTF. TOB. FCH. MATY. £750 ONO

FINANCE AVAILABLE SUBJECT TO STATUS

UNDERSTANDING THE ADVERTS — SOME COMMONLY USED ABBREVIATIONS

SOTE = Salt Of The Earth, *NS* = Non-Smoker, *NASF* = Non-Alvin Stardust Fan, *FCOB* = Full Control Of Bladder, *MNC* = Makes Nice Cakes, *SD* = Strict Disciplinarian, *DW* = Does Washing, *FSIP* = Fine to be Seen In Public, *PPAO* = Prone to getting the Photo Album Out, *STYHLG* = Still Thinks You're Her Little Girl, *WTC* = Wears Trendy Clothes, *SETYF* = Says Embarrassing Things To Your Friends, *CCF* = Cries at Crap Films, *LHA* = Looks Her Age, *LY* = Looks Younger, *EF* = Embarrassingly Frisky, *H* = Hairy, *CP* = Cheap Perfume,

TOB = Tolerant of Oafish Boyfriends, *OP* = Over-Protective, *SD* = Slight Dribble, *OT* = Own Teeth, *EBCRF* = Ex-Bay City Rollers Fan, *HL* = Hard Life, *POS* = Partial to Occasional Sherry, *DYAA* = Drive You Anywhere Anytime, *OV* = On Valium, *OP* = On Prozac, *OW* = On the Wagon, *FCH* = Fancies Charlton Heston, *WSITE* = Watches Stars In Their Eyes, *IB* = Insists on Baths, *WG* = Wants to be a Grandmother, *PF* = Plays Favourites, *MATY* = More Attractive Than You, *NHIL* = Never Had an Inside Loo

81

Surfing the Girl Power Vibe in a vibratiously Spice-O-Sphere way! What does it mean, exactly?

GIRL POWER IS A TOTALLY HAPPENING, TOTALLY HONEST, ZESTFUL, MEGADACIOUS WICKED PSYCHED-UP ASTEREOTYPICAL SOUL-EMPATHY RAP! IT'S A RESPECTFUL, UNIFYING CARING SOLIDARITY INDEPENDENT VIBE. IT'S COMPROMISE FREE, ADDED-VALUE, IMPULSIVE AND RESPECTFUL! IT'S A DEAD COOL, FAB, FAST AND FURIOUS FEMALE FUTURE! IT'S TIMELESS, RIGHT NOW, RETRO 90S. IT'S A RADICAL NO SURRENDER, AUTONOMISTIC, ALL-WIN, LAY DOWN, STAND UP, ATTITUDINALLY EQUALITIFIC KICKING LIFE GROOVE. IT'S A RELIGIOUSLY EXISTENTIAL MONSTER ARCHETYPICALLY GENDER-CENTRIC, LARGE LIVING UNIFYING, TRUTH-BOND. IT'S NOW. IT'S THEN. IT'S AS IT EVER WAS. IT'S AS IT SHALL BE. IT'S A FUNNY COLOUR BUT WE CAN RE-PAINT IT. IT'S ABOUT GETTING REAL AND LIVING LARGE IN A SELF-RELIANT, CARING, SHARING, FEMALE-ORIENTATED NON-JUDGEMENTAL CONTROL-FREAK NEXT GENERATION SORT OF WAY. IT'S AN EU RATIFIED, SPIRIT-FREEING, SOUL-CAPTURING, METAPHYSICAL, REALISTIC, PREJUDICIALLY NEGATORY, SEASONALLY ADJUSTED MOTHER LOVING, SELF-BELIEF, OBJECTIVE MIND-SET THAT TELLS IT HOW IT IS AND SAYS YO! RESPECT! TO THE INDIVIDUALISTIC VIBE AND ALL OUR FANS OUT THERE. AND OUR MUMS. IT'S GIRL POWER. NOT ONLY THAT. IT'S 100% PURE SOMETHING. AND THAT SOMETHING IS SPICE!

Other types of Power that are nowhere as brilliant as Girl Power!

Solar Power
Wind Power
Flower Power
Hydroelectric Power
Nuclear Power
Battery Power
Prince and the New Power Generation
Turtle Power

DID YOU KNOW?: #9

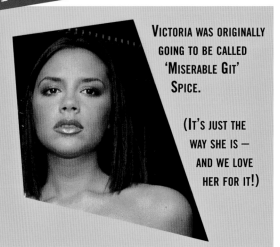

VICTORIA WAS ORIGINALLY GOING TO BE CALLED 'MISERABLE GIT' SPICE.

(IT'S JUST THE WAY SHE IS — AND WE LOVE HER FOR IT!)

Spice Merchandise!

IN NEED OF SMALL TABLES BUT STRAPPED FOR SPACE? DON'T WORRY! WITH THE NEW SPICE GIRLS NEST OF TABLES

THIS IS NOT A TOY

2 BECOME 1!

USING SPACE AGE TECHNOLOGY, 2 TABLES CAN TAKE UP THE SPACE OF 1!

MANUFACTURED FROM NATURAL, LIGHTWEIGHT TEAK, THIS NEST OF TABLES MAKES AN ATTRACTIVE AND PRACTICAL ADDITION TO ANY LIVING ROOM.

DOLPHIN FRIENDLY!

£59.99 FOR TWO (BUT THEY TAKE UP THE SPACE OF JUST ONE!)

I've heard that Iran has its own version of the Spice Girls. Is this true?

SUBMISSIVE SHI'ITE

SERVILE SHI'ITE

OBEDIENT SHI'ITE

Yes they're....

The Shi'ite Girls!

DOCILE SHI'ITE

SUBSERVIENT SHI'ITE

What does the application form for the Spice Girls look like?

SPICE GIRLS APPLICATION FORM

In completing this form, please do not use crayon. Answer ALL questions, especially the one about your weight. Marks will be deducted for correct spelling and punctuation.

Name:
Address: Miss/Ms/Mrs:
Postcode:
                     Daytime Tel No:

Age: Colour of Hair: Condition of teeth:

What Spice Name have you thought up for yourself? (Please do not use 'Sexy Spice'. We get 400 applications a day from Sexy Spice)
.... Spice

That's too rude. Think of another one:
.... Spice

Can you sing?
[ ] Yes [ ] No

Can you dance?
[ ] Yes [ ] No

What is your present weight?
...st ...lbs

Are you sure about that?
Oh, all right then ...st ...lbs

...We have sophisticated star-weighing devices...
...st ...lbs

How tall are you?
.........cm

...Without those huge wedges?
.........cm

Do you always do what you're told?
[ ] Yes [ ] No

Has anyone ever used the following phrases to describe you?
[ ] Argumentative [ ] On the ball [ ] Thoughtful
[ ] Financially astute [ ] Bright [ ] Not easily led
[ ] Trouble on legs [ ] Independent [ ] Very bright
[ ] Quiet [ ] Sensible [ ] Artistic and Creative

Do you think you will be able to get on with everyone in the band – even Victoria?
[ ] Yes [ ] No [ ] Everyone except Victoria

Are you likely to hit Victoria with your shoe if she keeps on getting up your nose?
[ ] Yes [ ] No

Have you ever been a man?
[ ] Yes [ ] No

Do you love your mum?
[ ] Yes [ ] No

Are you good at swearing?
[ ] Yes [ ] No

How would you best describe your accent?
[ ] Annoying Northern Twang [ ] Grating [ ] Dead common [ ] From the gutter
[ ] Primeval [ ] Incomprehensible [ ] Grange Hill

Can you wear inch thick make up without breaking out?
[ ] Yes [ ] No

What's more important to you?
[ ] Personal fulfilment [ ] Money
N.B. This is not a trick question

Would you be willing to pinch Prince Charles's bum if your PR man advised it?
[ ] Yes [ ] No [ ] I wouldn't go anywhere near that saggy old arse – or his bottom

Would you feel ashamed if someone else, possibly, possibly, wrote the songs but you got the credit?
[ ] Yes [ ] No

Surely you'd be offended if someone accused you of writing the lyrics for '2 Become 1'
[ ] Yes [ ] No [ ] A bit [ ] You can say I wrote 'Ra-Ra-Rasputin' if it gets me in the group

Are you likely to blow the whistle?
[ ] Yes [ ] No

Do you have any serious disabilities which may disqualify you from joining the group: e.g., big thighs, fat arse, dumpy bod, membership of Mensa, fashion sense, etc.
....

Finally, complete in your own words: 'I have a vibey groove because
....

Please list two references. One of which should be from someone under the age of eight and gullible and the other from someone who knows how things really work:
and...

I've completed my application form. Now what?

Rule One: Always send a polite covering letter with your official application form. Avoid being pushy or overly personal.

THE SPICE GIRLS

Dear Applicant,

I am writing to tell you that your application to join the Spice Girls has been unsuccessful.

Emma is a valued member of the band with her own legion of hardcore fans. We regret that we will not be inviting you to replace her. To do what you suggest would not only be illegal, it would be unsanitary.

Manager

P.S. I enclose a photo of Emma giving you the finger.

You will almost certainly be rejected at first. However, a true Spice Girl never gives up!

If at first you don't succeed, try and try again. You can improve your chances of joining the group by following these simple rules:

Rule Two: Do not include songs and lyrics with your application.

THE SPICE GIRLS

Dear Applicant

Thank you for your letter and your song. Yes, I think it is a very good song, but unfortunately it has already been written by Lennon and McCartney.

I am sorry that your application to join has been unsuccessful.

Manager

THE SPICE GIRLS

Dear Madonna,

Thank you for your application to join the group.
While I am sure that you would make an excellent member of the group and wouldn't mind making the tea and doing the girls' hair and cleaning up afterwards we have no vacancies at present.

Manager

P.S. You should spell your name with one 'D' and two 'Ns'.

Rule Four: Do not
attempt to bribe
your way in.

Rule Five: Don't be too
wacky or outrageous in an
attempt to get noticed.

THE SPICE GIRLS

Dear Applicant,

Returned herewith is your fiver and the photograph of yourself in a state of near undress.
I am sorry that I will not be able to take you up on your kind offer, but I have never liked fresh strawberries and I've got a bad back.

Manager

THE SPICE GIRLS

Dear Applicant,

While I'd agree that it's important to stand out and be noticed, submitting your application written in icing on the side of a donkey carcass delivered to my office accompanied by a singing midget did not work.
We already have one resident nutter in the group and I can just about deal with her. For this reason I am afraid to say that you have not been successful.

Manager

I know I won't get into the Spice Girls immediately after I finish reading this book. What should I do in the meantime?

Start your own girl group

While waiting for your chance to become a Spice, why not form your own band? It won't be as good as the Spice Girls of course – but who is? Forming your own band is simpler than you might imagine. All you have to do is...

- GET TOGETHER WITH SOME FRIENDS
- FIGHT OVER WHO'S GOING TO BE LEAD SINGER
- FIGHT OVER WHETHER YOU'RE GOING TO BE POP OR INDIE
- SPEND 99% OF YOUR TIME DESIGNING YOUR LOGO
- FIGHT OVER WHO'S GOING TO MARRY RONAN WHEN YOU MAKE IT AND YOU'RE FAMOUS
- TRY TO WRITE SONGS
- DECIDE TO DO COVERS INSTEAD
- DRIVE YOUR PARENTS INSANE DURING REHEARSALS IN THEIR SPARE ROOM
- FIGHT SOME MORE
- SPLIT UP

THAT'S ALL THERE IS TO IT! WHY NOT START TODAY!

Further education

Of course, you could always go back to school while waiting for your big break. It doesn't have to be maths and learning and boring stuff like that anymore! The colleges know that many people are intimidated by the term 'Higher Education' – so they've introduced 'Lower Education' to pack 'em in!

There are many courses you can choose from which will boost the skills you need to be in the Spice Girls when your chance arrives!

THE INSTITUTE OF LOWER EDUCATION
Honorary Patrons: the Spice Girls

BA (HONS) RAUCOUS
Includes modules in Yelling Skills, Waving Your Arms Energetically, Sheer Exuberance and Not Sitting Still.

MA ACTING THE PRAT
A newly introduced course. Core Subjects include Poor Drinking Skills, Talking Abject Rubbish and Pratting at Parties. Students are expected to be out every night and so fail to complete their thesis in time.

BA SHOUTING
Bellowing, Bawling, Shrieking and Screaming Your Lungs Out are all taught to degree level. Second year students will have a chance to shout in America thanks to our student exchange scheme.

BA FLATULENCE STUDIES (FORMERLY BA [HONS] SOCIOLOGY)
Students may choose between theoretical and practical options. N.B. This is a non-vocational course.

BA FAME
The ideal course for young people who still think they're destined to be more than office workers for their entire lives. You will be treated like demi-gods and allowed to develop specific skills in smugness, arrogance, rudeness and ingratitude. Students who successfully graduate will get a Batchelor's degree and a rude awakening.

SPECIAL DIPLOMA IN RUDE FACIAL GESTURES
Everything you could possibly need to know about how to be rude with your face. The Cocky Sneer, the Tongue Out and the Two Fingers Down the Throat are all covered. This is a popular course, so preference for places will be given to candidates who are long term unemployed or have heads. N.B. This diploma is recognized as a valid teaching qualification.

Oh, no! I've been rejected. Should I consider joining a rival band?

No. Nothing is as Spice-less as a Spice Girls bootleg band.

These sad Spice Girl wannabes live solely off myopic (or hard of hearing) girl group fans who think they're buying the real thing – not some purely cynical, image-based, hype-driven, marketing-lead commerical operation designed to separate fans from their hard-earned cash while ripping off the real Spice Girls vibe!

Watch out for these particularly sad examples!

THE NICE GIRLS
GROUP COMPRISES 'VERY' NICE, 'QUITE' NICE, 'EXTREMELY' NICE, 'RATHER' NICE AND 'JOLLY' NICE

THE RICE GIRLS
GROUP COMPRISES 'PILAU' RICE, 'BASMATI' RICE, 'BROWN' RICE, 'WHOLE GRAIN' RICE AND 'UNCLE BEN'S' RICE

THE LICE GIRLS
GROUP COMPRISES 'HEAD' LICE, 'PUBIC' LICE, 'BODY' LICE, 'HOG' LICE AND 'WOOD' LICE

THE VICE GIRLS
GROUP COMPRISES 'HARMLESS' VICE, 'MAJOR' VICE, 'SORDID' VICE, 'BLACK AND DECKER' VICE AND 'MIAMI' VICE

THE TWICE GIRLS
GROUP COMPRISES 'DOUBLE' TWICE, 'BINARY' TWICE, 'DUO' TWICE AND THE 'TWICE TWINS'

THE SLICE GIRLS
GROUP COMPRISES 'CREAM' SLICE, 'SMALL' SLICE, 'THIN' SLICE, 'MEDIUM' SLICE AND 'THICK' SLICE

THE MICE GIRLS
GROUP COMPRISES 'FIELD' MICE, 'HARVEST' MICE, 'DOR' MICE, 'HOUSE' MICE AND 'TIT' MICE

THE PRICE GIRLS
GROUP COMPRISES 'NICE' PRICE, 'HIGH' PRICE, 'SPECIAL' PRICE, 'UNBELIEVABLY LOW' PRICE AND 'OUR PRICE'

THE THRICE GIRLS
GROUP COMPRISES 'TRIO' THRICE, '2+1' THRICE, 'TRINITY' THRICE, 'TREBLE' THRICE AND 'TERTIARY' THRICE

They've given me a contract! What's a contract?

THE PERFORMER'S CONTRACT

Miss .... (hereafter called THE PERFORMER) hereby warrants that she has this power to enter into contract with The Management (hereafter called THE MANAGEMENT).

The Management agree to pay The Performer under terms of separate contract and to accept her as a member of the Spice Girls.

1. The Performer agrees to be a good girl and do as she's told.

2. The Performer agrees to say nice things about the Group's sponsors, Pepsi Cola, at all times — even if Pepsi does make her burp, fart, hiccup, put on weight or break out in spots. If The Performer prefers Coca-Cola, she is to keep her big trap shut.

3. The Performer agrees not to say anything vaguely intelligent in case she shows up the others.

4. The Performer agrees to appear on stupid vacuous German pop shows and do dumb interviews with feeble teen magazines she probably stopped reading when she was six.

5. The Performer agrees to her likeness being used on all manner of overpriced rubbish including dolls, lunch boxes, T-shirts, calendars, tazos, posters, postcards, badges and feminine hygiene products — and whatever else we can dream up to part them from their cash.

6. The Performer is not allowed to ask why Girl Power means acting like the worst of men.

7. The Performer agrees to say she is in complete control of her own life and making all the decisions at every opportunity. However, making a decision may constitute a sackable offence.

8. The Performer agrees not to embarrass the group by acting sensibly, refusing to strike degrading poses, wearing normal clothes, being quiet in a public place, etc. Failure to behave irrationally and irresponsibly may constitute a sackable offence.

9. Getting fat will constitute a termination of this contract.

10. The Performer agrees to do anything for press photographers. (Anything is hereby defined as anything.) If The Performer fails to generate at least three headlines a week, this contract may be terminated.

11. Notification of termination of contract will be by rumour, cold shoulder or by reading about it in the Sun.

Signed...
(for The Management)

Witnessed..Dated...............

Signed...
(for The Performer)

Witnessed..Dated...............

If you promote 'Girl Power', why are there so many men involved with the band?

Er...Oh dear. We don't have enough space to answer that question.

Yes you do. You've got a whole page left.
Oh yes...so we do.

So tell us. If Girl Power means that girls can do anything they want, why do men do all the important jobs connected with the Spice Girls?
Er...we don't know what you mean.

Well, it was a bloke who got the band together in the first place, wasn't it?
Um...yes.

And it's a bloke who manages them?
That's true.

The people who co-write their records are men, aren't they?
Yes.

And what about the producer. He's a man, isn't he?
Yes.

And the sound engineer. Another bloke?
Yep.

And the musicians. Aren't they all men?
True enough.

What about the person who promotes the tours. He's a man too, right?
Yes.

And the tour manager? Another bloke?
As such, I suppose so.

And the video director? A man?
There's no pulling the wool over your eyes, is there?

And I bet the person who filmed it was a cameraman?
True. But he could pass for a woman – quite easily – if he was made-up and took the beard off...

And the record pluggers. Women?
Guess again.

Men?
Yes.

And what about the record company boss. He's a man as well?
Technically.

What does that mean?
Yes.

OK. What about the marketing director. He must be a man.
No.

The marketing director's NOT a man?
No. He is a man. I was bluffing but I didn't manage to pull it off.

And what about the publicity manager. Another man?
Right again.

And the press agent. Someone of the male gender, perhaps?
Can't fault you there.

I bet there's absolutely no women involved with the band, their management or the record company at all!
Actually, there is one woman.

Oh, really. And what does she do?
She cleans the recording studio.

How Do I Get A Great Spicy Autograph Like The Girls?

Imagine someone wants your autograph! Of course, they don't at the moment because you're nobody – but when you join the Spice Girls you won't be so worthless any more!

Start practising your own unique Spice siggy right now. And if you haven't any ideas about how to design it, here's the girls' real-life xtra-Spicey sigs to inspire you...

GERI'S THE HOT AND PASSIONATE ONE OF THE GROUP, SO SHE JUST SIGNS HER NAME WITH A BIG KISS!

VICTORIA'S SULTRY AND MYSTERIOUS — SO SHE ALWAYS SIGNS HER NAME WITH AN ENIGMATIC CROSS.

MEL B IS A FAN OF THE FAMOUS CIVIL RIGHTS LEADER MALCOLM X, SO SHE SIGNS HER NAME AS A TRIBUTE TO HIM.

MEL C DECIDED TO DO HER SIGNATURE A LITTLE DIFFERENT SO IT WOULDN'T GET CONFUSED WITH MEL B'S. OOPS!

EMMA SIGNS HER NAME LIKE THIS.

GOOD THINGS TO WRITE IN FANS' AUTOGRAPH BOOKS

- IT'S A GIRL'S WORLD
- SISTERS ARE DOIN' IT FOR THEMSELVES!
- WOMEN ARE WINNIN'!
- IT'S A GIRL THANG!
- THE FUTURE IS FEMALE
- DO IT, SISTAH!
- GIRL POWER!
- LUV YA!
- GO FOR IT!
- ZIGAZIG-HA!

BAD THINGS TO WRITE IN FANS' AUTOGRAPH BOOKS

- I hate you!
- Thanks for the cash!
- Get a life!
- Lose weight!
- Thanks for being so gullible!
- Bet you wish you were me!
- Change that face!
- To the girl in the cheap clothes!
- Hello nobody
- I think you're really brave to wear those glasses
- To ugly, with love
- Do you know you dribble when you're excited?

SPICE GIRLS COLLECTION

Name . . . . (PLEASE USE BLOCK CAPITALS)

Address . . . .

. . . . Postcode . . . .

IF PAYING BY VISA /ACCESS, WRITE YOUR CARD NO. HERE: EXPIRY DATE: SIGNATURE:

. . . .

How to order

Ordering is easy. It's affording everything you want that's difficult! Get someone who went to school before comprehensive education to help you complete this form. And don't forget to add postage and packing or you'll get a tart note from us. And the Girls won't like you.

	ITEM	CODE	PRICE £	QUANTITY	TOTAL £
1	Spice Girls White Plastic Bum Bag	SG12	£19.99		
2	Spice Girls Broken Pencil	SG14	£3.99		
3	Spice Girls Hedge Strimmer	SG18	£39.99		
4	Spice Girls 'How To Shout' book	SG21	£7.50		
5	Spice Girls Empty Crisp Packet	SG23	£1.99		
6	Spice Girls Nothing	SG31	£9.99		
7	Spice Girls Tofu Boil-In-The-Bag Supreme (1kg)	SG32	£5.49		
8	Spice Girls Rancid Badger Vomit (6 fluid ounces)	SG34	£19.50		
9	Spice Girls Home Chutney Repair Kit	SG36	£12.00		
10	Spice Girls Bit Of String	SG37	£1.50		
11	Spice Girls Hedgehog Disguise Kit	SG39	£24.99		
12	Spice Girls Splinter (insert under skin – works immediately)	SG40	£6.25		
13	Spice Girls Offal and Giblet Sculpting Set	SG45	£65.50		
14	Spice Girls Spittoon (stainless steel, featuring Eternal)	SG46	£17.99		
15	Spice Girls Potato Peeler-cum-Toe Nail Trimmer	SG47	£8.99		
16	Spice Girls Plank of Wood (2m x 20cms x 3cms)	SG52	£3.00		
17	Spice Girls Fart Powder	SG56	£2.99		
18	Spice Girls Guide to the Battlefields of France	SG58	£7.99		
19	Spice Girls Musical Kagoules (XL only)	SG59	£32.00		
20	Spice Girls PartyFun Tea Caddy	SG64	£12.99		
21	Spice Girls Incontinent Otter	SG66	£75.00		
22	Spice Girls Big Exploding Thing	SG67	£24.99		
23	Spice Girls Slimy Thing That Goes Squeak When You Tread On It	SG70	£4.99		
24	Spice Girls Sloth Lingerie (one size fits all)	SG74	£24.99		

P & P	£2.95
GRAND TOTAL	

WARNING

Unofficial merchandise is neither made to the same high quality standards and/or subjected to the same high mark-up. It is also cursed and anyone buying it will have bad luck for the rest of their lives and will never get a boyfriend. Ever. Unofficial merchandise has also been known to spontaneously combust and to carry the virulent Anthrax virus. If you have a friend who buys Unofficial Spice Girls merchandise, please tell them where they are going wrong. If they do not listen, slap them. In fact, you can buy the Spice Girls Friend Slapper (code SG 94) for just £11.99. You will be doing them a favour because people who have purchased Unofficial Spice Girls merchandise have been known to be eaten by wild dogs. That and fail all their GCSEs in a big way.

TWENTY THINGS THE SPICE GIRLS WILL ACHIEVE IN 1998: